SCHOOL OF ORIENTAL AND AFRICAN
University of London

C L I F F O R D   G E E R T Z   *by*   H I S   C O L L E A G U E S

CLIFFORD GEERTZ

HIS *by* COLLEAGUES

Edited by Richard A. Shweder

and Byron Good

The University of Chicago Press

Chicago and London

RICHARD A. SHWEDER is the William Claude Reavis
Distinguished Service Professor in the Committee on Human
Development at the University of Chicago, and a Carnegie
Scholar (2003).

BYRON GOOD is professor of medical anthropology and
chairman of the Department of Social Medicine at Harvard
University.

The University of Chicago Press, Chicago 60637
The University of Chicago Press, Ltd., London
© 2005 by The University of Chicago
All rights reserved. Published 2005
Printed in the United States of America

14 13 12 11 10 09 08 07 06 05   1 2 3 4 5
ISBN: 0-226-75609-2 (cloth)
ISBN: 0-226-75610-6 (paper)

Library of Congress Catalog-in-Publication Data

Clifford Geertz by his colleagues / edited by Richard A. Shweder and
Byron Good.
     p.   cm.
    Presentations at a symposium held Nov. 23, 2002 in New
Orleans, La., in celebration of the 100th year anniversary of the
formation of the American Anthropological Association.
    Includes bibliographical references and index.
    ISBN 0-226-75609-2 (cloth : alk. paper)—ISBN 0-226-75610-6
(pbk. : alk. paper)
    1. Geertz, Clifford—Congresses.   2. Anthropologists—United
States—Biography—Congresses.   3. Anthropologists—Asia—
Biography—Congresses.   I. Geertz, Clifford.   II. Shweder,
Richard A.   III. Good, Byron.
GN21.G44C53 2005
301'.092—dc22

                                  2004017205

Contents

Preface

THIS PREFACE INVITES THE READER to vicariously participate in a historic intellectual event. On November 23, 2002, on the occasion of the celebration of the 100th anniversary of the formation of the American Anthropological Association (AAA), the executive board of the Association sponsored a Presidential Session honoring "The Work and Life of Clifford Geertz." This event, a full afternoon symposium held in a ballroom at the Hyatt Hotel in New Orleans, Louisiana, was cosponsored by the Society for Psychological Anthropology and organized by the editors of this book. An overflowing audience listened to eleven presentations followed by a riveting response and commentary by Clifford Geertz, who has been the single most influential American anthropologist of the past four decades.

Geertz's writings (see appendix 2) have defined, exemplified, and given character and depth to the intellectual agenda of a meaning-centered, nonreductive "interpretive social science," and have provoked much excitement and debate about the nature of human understanding and its relationship to social science explanations. In 1970 he founded the School of Social Science at the Institute for Advanced Study in Princeton, New Jersey, which proved to be an ideal setting for the interdisciplinary articulation of his work, and where, although recently ascending to the status of the emeriti, he continues to be one of anthropology's greatest and brightest lights. Given the aims of the Presidential Session—to both honor Geertz's multifaceted academic career and critically engage his broad intellectual agenda—participants in the symposium included a historian (Natalie Davis); a psychologist (Jerome Bruner); experts on cultural locales where Geertz had done research, such as Morocco, Bali, and Java (James Boon, Dale Eickelman, James Peacock, Lawrence Rosen); and culture theorists, globalization theorists, and psychological anthropologists of various sorts and persuasions (Mary-Jo DelVecchio Good, Michael Fischer, Byron Good, Ulf Hannerz, Robert LeVine, and Richard Shweder). Due to a sudden but temporary illness the philosopher Amelie

Rorty was unable to present her paper at the symposium, but her contribution is made available in this book, as is Clifford Geertz's response to her essay (which he did not deliver at the symposium).

The organizers hoped to bring together Clifford Geertz and some of his most well known colleagues for a serious colloquy and reflection on the importance of his work. On that memorable afternoon in New Orleans Geertz's contribution to cultural anthropology was interrogated (and celebrated) from a variety of perspectives. The substance and style of his writings were analyzed, praised, and cross-examined. Several of the presenters invited him to clarify issues, ranging from questions about the local versus the global, about the opposition between relativism and absolutism, and about the Geertzian conception of human psychology and mental functioning. The afternoon was divided into two sections, with a fifteen-minute break in between. The speakers for each section sat at an elevated table, and in turn spoke from a podium to the very large and very crowded room. Geertz himself sat in one of the forward rows, but amongst the audience, until the expectant moment when he rose, walked forward to the podium, and offered a response.

He had received drafts of most of the papers in advance and carried in his hands a bunch of notes on what he had read and what he had just heard. In his informative, witty, and utterly engaging commentary, he addressed the central points in each and every presentation. He gave advice to younger generations of anthropologists and concluded by giving his blessings to the field of cultural psychology and by spelling out the essential features of his theory of symbolic action. The huge audience—which seemed to appreciate the substance of the proceedings, the brilliance and intellectual seriousness of the commentary, and the historic character of the event—responded to Geertz by jumping collectively to its feet, thereby concluding the symposium with a rousing standing ovation.

This slim volume is neither a videotape nor an audiotape—the sights and sounds of that dazzling, riveting, and ultimately inspiring academic occasion are now but memories in the minds of those who were fortunate enough to have experienced them firsthand. Nevertheless, this book does preserve the main intellectual record of that afternoon's interrogation and appreciation of the work and life of Clifford Geertz, along with his illuminating and stunning response. Although our "Cliff Notes" are meant to be a historical record of sorts, we should note that our table of contents is not identical to the order of presentations at the symposium (see appendix 1 for the original symposium schedule). Geertz's remarks are more or less unchanged from those he gave at the symposium, although hard copies of three of the papers were available only after the event, thus providing an opportunity for comment in slightly more detail. The ordering of Geertz's responses to particular presentations is faithful to the ordering of his remarks at the symposium. His remarks unfolded according to their own logical flow and pattern of cross-referencing, which were not designed to mirror the temporal sequence of the program schedule.

We wish to thank several people for their dedication to this project, most especially Michele Wittels, who contributed in innumerable ways to the organization of the symposium event and the preparation of this book. Our gratitude extends as well to Don Brenneis (president of the American Anthropological Association), and Deborah Heath (program chair for the 2002 American Anthropological Association meetings), for their enthusiastic sponsorship of the symposium as a featured event at the AAA meetings; and to Geoffrey White (president of the Society for Psychological Anthropology) and Robert Desjarlais (program chair for the Society for Psychological Anthropology), for their cosponsorship of this Presidential Session and appreciation of the proceedings. The University of Chicago Press and Clifford Geertz are both icons of scholarly greatness in anthropology, and we are most grateful to David Brent, the Press's brilliant editor, for supporting this project and making the match.

—Richard Shweder and Byron Good

Richard A. Shweder   I

Cliff Notes

The Pluralisms of Clifford Geertz

FOR THREE DECADES Clifford Geertz has been the single most influential cultural anthropologist in the United States. Throughout
his career he has put his vast intellectual and literary skills to work "fer-
reting out the singularities of other peoples' ways of life," cultivating a
provocative variety of philosophical pluralism and promoting the idea
that there is no fixed kernel to human nature. No "mind for all cultures."
No "deep down homo." "If anthropology is obsessed with anything," he
writes, "it is with how much difference difference makes" (2000, 197). He
goes on to say, "If you want a *good* rule-of-thumb generalization from
anthropology I would suggest the following: Any sentence that begins,
'All societies have . . .' is either baseless or banal" (135).

In many ways Cliff Geertz's sense of style has exemplified (and given
distinctive character) to his beliefs. He is a master of distinctions who
recoils at typologies, grand theories, and universal generalizations and rejects abstractionism and reductionism as methods for the social sciences.
He is a discriminating writer who feels very much at home taking the
measure of some complex scene. "Rushing to judgment," he writes, "is
more than a mistake, it's a crime" (2000, 45). He believes that ultimate
reality (if he is willing to speak of "ultimate" things at all) is a complex
continuum of overlapping likenesses and differences that should not be
placed in neat boxes, and certainly not two boxes. And as everyone in
this anthropological audience surely knows he is the mahatma of "thick
description." "I don't do systems," he writes, and his preference for portraying "cases," and his antipathy for general laws and formal principles
will be obvious to anyone familiar with his work.

Cliff Geertz's critics are many. Almost everyone initially gets side-
tracked by the visibility and distinctiveness of his writing style, which
is like Cyrano de Bergerac's nose. It is conspicuous, it is spectacular, but
it is best to just ignore it, for the sake of getting on with a discussion of his
ideas, which is what we hope to do in this symposium. Reading Clifford
Geertz is the perfect antidote to obscurantism in the social sciences, which

1

is a very good thing for those of us who have been educated, inspired, or challenged by his writings. It is even good for those who care to be constructive critics or to interrogate various aspects of his work.

Looking beyond reactions to style, it seems fair to say that among Geertz's critics the lumpers in the social sciences feel frustrated by him because he is a splitter who is not so easy to dismiss. He argues that knowledge is "local" and most social science generalizations restricted in scope, for which he has no regrets. Geertz writes, "I have never been able to understand why such comments as 'your conclusions, such as they are, only cover two million people [Bali], or fifteen million [Morocco], or sixty-five million [Java], and only over some years or centuries' are supposed to be criticisms" (2000, 137). Nevertheless, the universalizers mistakenly think he is a radical relativist. The positivists mistakenly think he is anti-science. And the skeptical postmodernists (by which I mean those scholars who really are subjectivists, nihilists, and radical relativists, which Clifford Geertz is not), think he is an old-fashioned American anthropologist who still believes there is some good work to be done with the idea of "culture" (by which I mean human conceptions of what is good, true, beautiful, and efficient made manifest, and thereby expressed, in practice).

But I am a fan. And one reason I admire his work so much is because I believe Cliff Geertz is one of the world's most significant proponents of cultural, moral, and scientific pluralism (which is not the same as radical relativism and is certainly not the same as being "anti-science").

If I had to identity some of the big philosophical or theoretical themes in his writings I would name four. Theme 1: Diversity is inherent in the human condition. Theme 2: There is no universal essence to human nature that *strongly* determines human behavior. Theme 3: Across time and space (history and culture) human nature is continuously transformed by the never-ending attempt of particular groups of human beings—Balinese, Moroccans, Northern European Protestants—to understand themselves and to create a social world that makes manifest their self-understandings. Theme 4: Securing universal agreement about what is good, true, beautiful, or efficient in life is rarely possible across cultures and, even more importantly, the ecumenical impulse to value uniformity (for example, convergence in belief) over variety and to overlook, devalue, or even eradicate "difference" is not a good thing. Culture is not icing, he writes. Biology is not cake. Differences are not necessarily shallow. Likeness is not necessarily deep (See Shweder 2000 for a similar but more expansive summary of Geertz's contribution to the social sciences).

Cliff Geertz has written that relativism "disables judgment" while absolutism "removes it from history." He has strongly intimated that finding a middle path between relativism and absolutism is what culture theory ought to be about. For my own very specific substantive contribution to this symposium I want to briefly focus on a not very small question concerning judgments about morality (good and bad, right and wrong) and on the issue of cultural critique. In particular I want to ask, is it possible to offer moral evaluations of the social practices of different societies without imposing one's own parochial or ethnocentric conception of things on others? If the answer is yes, precisely how is that to be done? If the answer is no, precisely why is that so? In other words, what exactly is Cliff Geertz's implied third choice between relativism and absolutism; and what exactly does it look like (what shape does it take) when one is asked to judge whether, for example, such customary practices as polygamy, arranged marriage, adolescent circumcision, physical punishment, animal sacrifice, and so forth are good or bad, right or wrong?

In his well-known essay "Anti Anti-Relativism," Cliff Geertz offers this quote from Montaigne: "Each man calls barbarism whatever is not his own practice . . . for we have no other criterion of reason than the example and idea of the opinions and customs of the country we live in." "That notion," Geertz then remarks, "whatever its problems, and however more delicately expressed, is not likely to go entirely away unless anthropology does" (2000, 45). He goes on to say, "What the relativists, so-called, want us to worry about is provincialism—the danger that our perceptions will be dulled, our intellects constricted, and our sympathies narrowed by the over-learned and overvalued acceptances of our own society" (45).

In the light of that remark it seems reasonable to raise the question: when it comes to evaluating the social norms of others what does the sharpening of our perceptions, the expanding of our intellects, and the widening of our sympathies actually amount to, and doesn't that process of sharpening, expanding, and widening imply that there is more to a moral judgment than Montaigne imagined? And if there is more, doesn't that process of informed evaluation take us beyond the country we live in, making it possible for us to achieve a nonethnocentric understanding of the degree of moral value of the customs of other societies. Doesn't the process of cultural critique mean that it is possible (perhaps difficult, but possible) to separate the provincial aspects from the nonprovincial aspects of ones own moral judgments?

My guess is that Cliff Geertz, for a variety of reasons (some of them

Wittgensteinian; some not), will be reluctant to theorize in the abstract about such questions. So in the little time that remains I aim to simply open a conversation, the ultimate purpose of which is to answer such questions. I would begin by inviting Cliff to say how his own position on moral judgment and cultural critique compares to the positions of two other famous anti-universalists from two other disciplines—the legal scholar Richard Posner and the philosopher Isaiah Berlin.[1]

Posner, who is a United States appellate judge and senior lecturer at the University of Chicago, is also the most widely cited contemporary American legal scholar. Notably, he is a thoroughgoing anti-realist and a provocative moral relativist. When it comes to the study of moral judgments he fully appreciates the Geertzian generalization that "Any sentence that begins, 'All societies have . . . is either baseless or banal.'" In his book *The Problematics of Moral and Legal Theory* (1999) he (Posner) quotes approvingly from Geertz's essay "Anti Anti-Relativism" and has the following to say:

> I shall be arguing first of all that morality is local, and that there are no *interesting* moral universals. There are tautological ones, such as "murder is wrong" where "murder" means "wrongful killing," or "bribery is wrong," where bribery means "wrongful paying." But what counts as murder, or as bribery, varies enormously from society to society. There are a handful of rudimentary principles of social cooperation—such as don't lie *all* the time or don't break promises without *any* reason or kill your relatives or neighbors indiscriminately—that may be common to all human societies, and if one wants to call these rudimentary principles the universal moral law, that is fine with me. But they are too abstract to be criterial. Meaningful moral realism is therefore out, and a form (not every form) of moral relativism is in. Relativism in turn invites an *adaptationist* conception of morality, in which morality is judged—nonmorally, in the way that a hammer might be judged well or poorly adapted to its goal of hammering nails into wood or plaster—by its contribution to the survival, or other ultimate goals, of a society or some group within it. Moral relativism implies that the expression "moral progress" must be used with great caution, because it is perspectival rather than objective; moral progress is in the eye of the beholder. (Posner 1999, 6)

In his book (an extension of his 1997 Oliver Wendell Holmes Lectures at Harvard University) Judge Posner offers a sustained attack on moral realism. In his lectures he suggests that "many moral claims are just the gift wrapping of theoretically ungrounded (and ungroundable) preferences and aversions." He also argues that if any nonlocal moral facts exist at all they are completely useless for resolving any actual real world moral issue. He writes,

> Every society, every subculture within a society, past or present, has had a moral code but a code shaped by the exigencies of life in that society or that subculture rather than by a glimpse of some overarching source of moral obligations. To the extent it is adaptive to those exigencies, the code cannot be criticized convincingly by outsiders. Infanticide is abhorred in our culture, but routine in societies that lack the resources to feed all children that are born. Slavery was routine when the victors in war could not afford to feed or free their captives, so that the alternative to enslaving them was killing them. Are infanticide and slavery "wrong" in these circumstances? It is provincial to say that "we are right about slavery, for example, and the Greeks wrong," so different was slavery in the ancient world from racial enslavement, as practiced, for example, in the United States until the end of the Civil War, and so different were the material conditions that nurtured these different forms of slavery. To call infanticide or slavery presumptively bad would be almost as provincial as unqualified condemnation. The inhabitants of an infanticidal or slave society would say with equal plausibility that infanticide or slavery is presumptively good, though they might allow that the presumption could be rebutted in peaceable, wealthy, technologically complex societies. (Posner 1999, 19)

Three features of Posner's position with regard to these and other cases are especially worthy of note. First, he describes himself as a moral relativist. As he stated in his Holmes Lectures he believes "that the criteria for pronouncing a moral claim valid are local, that is, are relative to the moral code of the particular culture in which the claim is advanced, so that we cannot call another 'immoral' unless we add 'by our lights.'"

Second, he allows that he is a moral subjectivist in the sense that he believes that there are no "reasonably concrete transcultural moral truths." In effect he argues that there is no independent or transcendent or objective domain of the right and the true (no "objective order of goodness") to which one might appeal, as the legitimate source for one's particular judgments about what is right or wrong, good or bad. (The discourse of "inalienable" or "natural" rights is, of course, by Posner's anti-realist account, thereby rendered either illusory or vacuous.)

Third, he claims that he is not a strong moral skeptic. There are moral truths worth knowing and judgments worth making, he argues. But they are merely facts about what is judged right and wrong in one's own society, for example, the existing social norms, customs, and laws of one's own land. These local norms and laws are knowable, he argues, and he is quite prepared to make parochial judgments about what is right and wrong for members of his parish or community, and to enforce them.

What Posner is not prepared to do is pretend that his judgments about the practices of other societies are anything more than reactions based on feelings of personal disgust. Perhaps as a result of personal temperament or cultural taste he might feel revolted by some practice (such as infanticide or suttee) and even inclined to intervene to stop the practice with the power at his command. Nevertheless he argues, in keeping with his anti-realist approach, "moral emotions" (shame, guilt, disgust, indignation) have no universal concrete moral content or objective foundation or source in some transcendental domain of the moral good.

Fully consistent with his moral subjectivism, he also rejects that idea that there is a universal moral obligation to tolerate cultures that have social norms different from one's own. He comes close to saying that the experience of a negative-feeling state may result in the exercise of power to eradicate the practices of others, and that it is misguided to even ask whether such an intervention is justifiable or not. The moral domain by Richard Posner's account of moral relativism and subjectivism is simply a natural scene in which different groups, each with their own distinctive social norms and equipped (in varying degrees) with powers and resources to dominate the local or global scene, compete with each other to perpetuate their own way of life. Some will succeed better than others do. Some will adapt or surrender their social norms under pressure to do so. But none of this social norm competition or social norm replacement represents true moral progress, and there are no rational discussions or arguments to be had about what the outcome of the competition or conflict ought to be. Why? Because, according to Posner, there is no objective moral standard against which divergent claims about what is right and good can be assessed. All that matters is power and the struggle to carry forward one's way of life efficiently, and to survive in the competition with other groups.

Precisely how do Cliff Geertz's views on these issues differ from Posner's, if at all? The comparison of Geertz and Posner is instructive. If I understand him correctly, Cliff Geertz believes that is it possible to reject subjectivism and radical relativism while at the same time refusing to place anything (other than banalities) outside of culture. Yet if I understand Posner correctly, he advocates moral subjectivism and relativism precisely because (Geertz-like) he refuses to place anything other than banalities outside of culture. Posner thereby forces us to ask the following question: If, as Cliff Geertz suggests, there is so very little in the moral domain that transcends culture and history, how it is possible for others to be both different from us in their social norms yet *entitled* to have their social norms valued by us, or at least tolerated by us, at the same time? Posner's version of anti-universalism (and his refusal to endorse tolerance or any other moral values as real or objective goods) provokes us to consider the possibility that a fully theorized stance of moral pluralism in anthropology must take us beyond any particular culture and outside of history, for the sake of the theory's own systematic justification. If one rejects both subjectivism and relativism, as Clifford Geertz (in apparent contrast to Richard Posner) recommends, what does one put in its place? In the absence of any objective values or nonethnocentric moral goods what type of value judgments survive the corrosive force of moral skepticism?

These are big questions, old questions, hard questions. Yet it is with regard to such questions that a comparison of Clifford Geertz to Isaiah Berlin is instructive. One wonders, how close is the connection between the Geertzian practice of anthropology and the philosophical theory of "value pluralism" elucidated by Berlin, and systematized in a thoughtful book by John Gray titled *Isaiah Berlin* (1996; also see Galston 2002). Berlin's theory is associated with the idea (quoting John Gray here and below) that "human values are objective but irreducibly diverse." And it is linked to an intellectual stance that affirms the "reality, validity and human intelligibility of values and forms of life very different from our own." One basic claim of the theory is that "fundamental human values are many, that they are often in conflict and rarely, if ever, necessarily harmonious, and that some at least of these conflicts are among incommensurables—conflicts among values for which there is no single, common standard of measurement or arbitration."

In other words some moral dilemmas are insolvable and ultimately undecidable by rational reflection. For Berlin at least that is not quite the same as saying (Montaigne-like) that there is nothing more to moral evaluation than "the opinions and customs of the country we live in" or (Posner-like) that moral judgments are no more than an expression of culturally socialized preferences and aversions. What would Cliff Geertz say about Berlin's theory of "value pluralism"? Would he accept that moral values (e.g., liberty, justice, loyalty, equality, protection of the vulnerable, beneficence) are not only diverse and irreconcilable but also real and objective (and in that sense *do* stand outside of culture and history)?

In one sense or another Clifford Geertz, Richard Posner, and Isaiah Berlin are all deeply critical of universalized moral claims about the goodness or badness, rightness or wrongness of particular social practices. They have views of moral value that appear to be similar in some ways and different in other ways. If I understand them correctly all three would argue that as a matter of fact people around the world do not universally agree on what behaviors in particular are right or wrong, good or bad. All three accept the notion that there exist moral disagreements that cannot (even in principle) be settled by rational means, and that to the extent there exist universal maxims of morality (for example, the injunction to be fair minded in the sense of treating like cases alike and different cases differently) those maxims cannot in and of themselves resolve real world moral disputes. All three would presumably argue that moral judgments depend on circumstances. I can only guess whether Cliff Geertz would accept Posner's argument that there is no such thing as objective moral progress. I can only speculate whether he would accept Posner's view that even the presumption that infanticide is immoral is too presumptive and provincial to count as a moral universal; although I suspect that he would endorse the stance advocated by both Posner and Berlin that there is no determinate or universal way to choose between various alternative moral claims, for example claims of autonomy versus community, or liberty versus equality, or family values versus sexual pleasure? But I would certainly love to hear some of his answers to such questions.

A systematic comparison of Geertz's theory of value with the value theories of Posner and Berlin is sure to be helpful in the further development of a philosophically defensible anthropological theory of cultural pluralism. And it is one very timely way to be challenged by, and to honor, that great intellectual tradition that extends from Franz Boas to Clifford Geertz. I have been speaking here, of course, of an intellectual tradition that (not by coincidence) is coincidental with the 100-year-old history of the American Anthropological Association itself. And, I might add, in a world in which triumphal "West Is Best" thinking has returned in full force to the international scene, it is an intellectual and critical tradition that is just as important today as it was in 1902, during a former age of global empire.

NOTE

1. A more extensive discussion of Posner and Berlin appears in a keynote address, "The Idea of Moral Progress: Bush versus Posner versus Berlin," which I delivered at the 2003 Philosophy of Education Society meetings. Parts of that discussion are reported here as well.

Also see Richard A. Schweder, "Moral Realism without the Ethnocentrism: Is It Just a List of Empty Truisms?" in *Human Rights with Modesty: The Problem of Universalism*, ed. András Sajó (Leiden: Martinus Nijhoff Publishers, 2004).

REFERENCES

Galston, William A. 2002. *Liberal Pluralism: The Implications of Value Pluralism for Political Theory and Practice*. New York: Cambridge University Press.

Geertz, Clifford. 2000. *Available Light: Anthropological Reflections on Philosophical Topics*. Princeton: Princeton University Press.

Gray, John. 1996. *Isaiah Berlin*. Princeton: Princeton University Press.

Posner, Richard A. 1999. *The Problematics of Moral and Legal Theory*. Cambridge: Harvard University Press.

Shweder, Richard A. 2000. The Essential Anti-Essentialist. Review of Clifford Geertz, *Available Light: Anthropological Reflections on Philosophical Topics*. *Science* 290 (November 24): 1511–12.

Passing Judgment

Interpretation, Morality, and Cultural
Assessment in the Work of Clifford Geertz

I N THE PREFACE TO *AVAILABLE LIGHT*, Clifford Geertz lists the issues he has sought to pursue empirically as "the role of ideas in behavior, the meaning of meaning, the judgment of judgment."[1] "Judgment,"
of course, implies a wide range of practices. Although some anthropologists have spoken of "sick societies" and many others clearly have their
own assessment of the people they study (as do the "natives" of them,
there also being much truth in the old saw that "every anthropologist
gets the society he or she deserves"), most anthropologists do not—or at
least they usually pretend they do not—judge other cultures in the sense
of forming an opinion or conclusion about them.[2] At best the judgmental
anthropologist may be more akin to a self-appointed referee engaged in
authoritative guesswork even though the people studied may view the
meaning of "judgment" as applied to anthropological writings as more
like a misfortune inflicted through no fault of their own.

But these are not, of course, the senses of judgment to which Geertz is
referring. Rather his is a very subtle blend of studying the ways in which
others go about creating and comparing the construction of their own
experience at the same time that, without literally adjudging them, the
ethnographer does not remain impervious to the implications of their actions. Three elements thus converge in this regard in Geertz's approach
as an ethnographer, elements that may be posed as a set of interrelated
questions. The first is really about articulating our own scholarly standards, for it asks: If ethnography is to be an interpretive enterprise what
criteria should be used to assess interpretations not as right or wrong but
rather as better or worse? Second, if interpretation does import at least
relative standards, in what sense is interpretation a moral act, one that
necessarily carries some implications of desirable conduct? And, finally,
these questions allow the possibility for the third, more directly judgmental question, by asking: In at least implicitly establishing such criteria does

Geertz's work, though that is certainly not its primary aim, point to ways in which we can also set some of the terms for the judgment of other cultures and our own? Let me take each of these issues in turn.

Geertz does not give us a separate programmatic statement about how to tell better from worse interpretations. His approach, as in all such matters, is informed by his belief that one demonstrates the value of a theory by what it shows us about its subject, by its capacity to capture particularity as part of general propositions. "Theory . . . grows out of particular circumstances and, however abstract, is validated by its power to order them in their full particularity, not by stripping the particularity away" (Geertz, *Available Light,* 2000 [hereafter AL], 138).[3] Like William James (and unlike, say, Ernest Gellner), Geertz is a not a monist but a pluralist. He rejects (as one commentator has said of James) "the specious consolation and aesthetic charm of the former for the real moral challenge of the latter."[4] Rejecting the "tendency to see diversity as surface and universality as depth" (AL, 59) in favor of the idea that "difference must be seen *not* as the negation of similarity" but as "comprising it: locating it, concretizing it, giving it form" (226–27, original italics), Geertz asks us to appreciate that the "enormous number of similar intersections of outlook, style, or disposition, are the bases on which cultural complexity is ordered into at least something of an irregular, rickety, and indefinite whole" (254–55). Not all approaches, therefore, would seem to be equally meritorious in showing how such specific conceptual and relational patterns "come to have the force, the immediacy, and the consequences they have" (211), how they constitute a "system" that is, to borrow George Kateb's phrasing from a different context, "not so much believable as capable of being believed in by others."[5] Thus when he speaks of the "virtues of a 'local knowledge' sort of tack" (137) Geertz lists "knowledge of limits" (the rejection of authority "that comes from nowhere"), coupled with highly circumstantial accounts, comparisons that bring out contrasts and particularities (137–38), and a "grasp of the moral and political issues involved" as factors that, whatever else, may yield an account that is "surer, less prey to the confusing noises of the confused present."[6] The idea that a culture may constitute a highly structured configuration or just "a bundle of parochialisms that somehow adheres" (255) also bears on the connection between the aesthetics of a better interpretation and the moral aspects of the process of interpretation itself.

Scientists have used replication and Occam's Razor, social scientists have spoken of elegance and parsimony, humanists have applied notions of validity based on comprehensiveness and authorial intent—all of them

means of trying to achieve criteria for interpretation.[7] Each involves a
certain aesthetic and Geertz would, I think, agree with Isaiah Berlin's position (following Vico and Herder) that cultures, being incommensurable,
require us to attend to their coherence without being censorious, to see
the creativity of particular forms and styles as central.[8] Thus Geertz can
criticize Cai Hua, who claims that the Na of China exhibit no forms of
marital alliance or descent, because "we hear little of the tone and temper
of Na life, of the color of their disposition, the curve of their experience."[9]
But he departs quite crucially from Berlin in that he does not think this
places the understanding of cultures beyond moral evaluation.[10] To the
contrary, the place of morality in interpretation is crucial to Geertz's own
interpretive turn.

The act of interpretation is a moral act twice over for Geertz. It in-
corporates, first, the scholar's involvement with others in casting up an
understanding of their lives and in taking actions that will affect one another's well being.[11] And it is also a moral act to engage in the interpretation of one's own and others' morality itself. Thus, in the first instance
the anthropologist must "look at persons and events (and at oneself) with
an eye at once cold and concerned," realizing that "Detachment comes
not from a failure to care, but from a kind of caring resilient enough
to withstand an enormous tension between moral reaction and scientific
observation, a tension which only grows as moral perception deepens
and scientific understanding advances" (AL, 40). And in the second instance, one cannot leave matters at the descriptive level of a "plurality of
incommensurable cultures."[12] The act of interpretation involves not only
deciding what something is but, as Geertz's colleague Michael Walzer has
argued, how to respond to the question "What is the right thing *for us*
to do?"[13] Like deciding what the law should be by portraying what the
law is, or appraising the practices of a culture in terms of the effects of
some people's acts on others, interpretation necessarily includes moral
decision-making. "Deprived of a yardstick, [writes Walzer, in a vein that
is certainly Geertzian] we rely on exegesis, commentary, and historical
precedent, a tradition of argument and interpretation."[14] And as we give
an account of any system of morality we necessarily give an account of
our own that must intersect that of the others we address.

So, in the words of the medieval Welsh bard: "You must judge at the
end."[15] If some of the criteria for judgment—of the quality of interpretations, of the merit of a particular moral stance, of what we make of
ourselves in the process of assessing other—appear at times vague or resis-
tant to replication, that may, for Geertz, be related to his view of both our

capabilities as scholars and social life itself. "The puzzles of judgment," as he calls them,[16] bring together the uncertainties and ambiguities of social life with the limits of our own insights. Like Aristotle, who took it as the hallmark of a mature man that he did not try to describe an entity with greater precision than the thing itself possessed, or the later Wittgenstein, who said one should not try to depict a cloud with sharp lines, or unlike Ruth Benedict, who, no doubt unintentionally, demonstrated that by "trying too hard to be clear . . . [one] can dim an argument best left oblique,"[17] Geertz seeks the appropriate measure of specificity for capturing the specific. Like Aristotle, too, he believes that political theory should (among other things) be a school for judgment, and that our own politics in a diverse world require a "unity of intent" (AL, 257) and "a liberalism with both the courage and the capacity to engage itself with a differenced world" (259).

To pursue simultaneously the understanding and the assessment of judgment nevertheless poses difficult professional and personal questions. Geertz is, as I have suggested, saying that we cannot judge other cultures as anthropologists. But we certainly can as individuals. This position does, however, present a dual dilemma. First, it means we cannot formulate with certainty criteria that would allow us to rely on anthropological data to reach any judgmental position. We may know that race does not correlate with social complexity or that gender and caste do not correlate with intellectual ability. In the absence of judgmental absolutes, however, we would only interfere with our primary task as anthropologists—namely, to understand how others' ideas and practices fit into their own sociocultural lives—if we let the belief that we could ultimately judge others predominate.[18] But there is also a second dilemma; namely, that even in our role as anthropologists we may not be able to use the insights of moral judgment to assess what is taking place in the subject culture if, lurking in the distance, there remains the expectation of ultimate judgments. A kind of anthropological uncertainty principle, akin to that developed in physics by Heisenberg, may be at work. We cannot as anthropologists make supportable moral judgments and simultaneously have the highest confidence in our ability to study the meaning people attribute to their own thoughts and acts.[19] Both perspectives may yield worthwhile insights, but in pursuing one perspective some uncertainty is necessarily introduced into the other. In short, what we can do as anthropologists is to look at how the people we study judge judgment. We cannot as anthropologists exercise absolute judgment over their judgment.

In Geertz's view, anthropology can nevertheless improve, even though it cannot prescribe, our personal appraisals—but only to the extent that it is grounded on adequate knowledge and humility. "We must learn to grasp what we cannot embrace," he says (AL, 87); "to judge without understanding constitutes an offense against morality" (40); and, indeed, "rushing to judgment is more than a mistake, it's a crime" (45).[20] His position appears similar to that of one writer who has said, apropos one of Geertz's favorite topics: "You have to pick your place to stand, and work by the light of informed intellect, before you can judge whether social institutions or indeed whole societies are accreting meaning or leaking it away."[21] The result is hardly moral paralysis. Geertz would, I think, agree with the film critic Pauline Kael, who wrote that "A mistake in judgment isn't fatal, but too much anxiety about judgment is."[22] Judgment of self and others, necessarily entangled in the anthropological enterprise, cannot be totally avoided, but ought not, Geertz makes clear, to be the first or indeed the last reason for our studies. For him, anthropology is, therefore, neither a terrain for the enactment of what I would call "the higher personal politics" nor an invitation to mindless relativism.[23]

Accordingly, Geertz has not shrunk from making clearly judgmental statements when, for example, he speaks of people in the Third World for whom the problem is sometimes "not what to believe but how to believe it," or who display, in his view, great uncertainty over what, if any, meaning to assign to various aspects of their lives.[24] Similarly, on the political level, it is sometimes insufficiently appreciated how Geertz has spoken out about the massacres in Bali and Java in the 1960s, or the political limitations of the regime of the Moroccan King Hassan II, and he has certainly been modest about the work he has done with the National Academy of Sciences on behalf of imprisoned Indonesian intellectuals.[25] It is, to borrow the title of one of his most important writings on this subject, that "Thinking as a Moral Act" is made all the more difficult and all the less avoidable when one attends to the profound differences among human cultures. To read his detailed ethnographies or his most theoretical of analyses without grasping the reasons why, for him, morality and judgment suffuse his concerns, even when his judgments are neither trumpeted nor self-referring, would, therefore, be to miss one of the most essential aspects of his entire life's work.

Finally, on a somewhat personal note, I may very well be the only person who has ever bought a used car from Cliff Geertz. Now the purchase of a used car from one's teacher certainly constitutes an act of interpersonal trust and moral engagement, to say nothing of a source for intellectual speculation. Future biographers may, therefore hotly debate the role of this car in the formation of Geertz's thought and (rather less hotly, I suspect) my own. Some may see in his offer of the car to me the inspiration for his theory of the symbol as a "material vehicle of thought" while others, seeing it from the perspective of a hard-pressed graduate student who was getting a good deal, as contributing to my own view of certain symbols as "a thoughtful vehicle of materialism." Admittedly, that 1964 Simca probably did little to inspire some of Geertz's more important theoretical insights. It wasn't much of a "model of" much less a "model for" anything, including the vaunted accomplishments of the automaker's art. But the car got him and later me where we were going. So for the good deal, the memorable moments of those few months we overlapped in the field, and for so much else before and since, I am, like all those within and beyond the academy, deeply indebted to Cliff Geertz—for his insights, his generosity, and, not least, for the self-effacing brilliance of his own judgment of judgment.

NOTES

1. Clifford Geertz, *Available Light: Anthropological Reflections on Philosophical Topics*, Princeton: Princeton University Press, 2000, x.

2. On the idea of "sick societies" see, for example, Robert B. Edgerton, *Sick Societies* (New York: Maxwell Macmillan International, 1992); and Raoul Narroll, "Cultural Determinants and the Concept of the Sick Society," in *Changing Perspectives in Mental Illness,* ed. Stanley C. Plog and Robert B. Edgerton (New York: Holt, Rinehart and Winston, 1969), 128–55.

3. "What we need, it seems, are not enormous ideas, nor the abandonment of synthesizing notions altogether. What we need are ways of thinking that are responsive to particularities, to individualities, oddities, discontinuities, contrasts, and singularities, responsive to what Charles Taylor has called 'deep diversity,' a plurality of ways of belonging and being, and that yet can draw from them—from it—a sense of connectedness, a connectedness that is neither comprehensive nor uniform, primal nor changeless, but nonetheless real" (AL, 224).

4. Houston Peterson, introducing James's essay "On a Certain Blindness in Human Beings," in *Essays in Philosophy*, ed. Houston Peterson (New York: Pocket Books, 1959), 263. Peterson goes on to describe James's position (and to quote internally James's "The Dilemma of Determinism," from *The Will to Believe and Other Essays in Popular Philosophy*, ed. Frederick H. Burkhardt, Fredson Bowers, and Ignas K. Skrupskelis [Cambridge: Harvard University Press, 1979], 177): "[James] admitted that his 'pluralistic, restless universe, in which no single point of view can ever take in the whole scene' would have no appeal 'to a mind possessed of the love of unity at any cost.' " "A friend with such a mind once told me [James writes] that the thought of my universe made him sick, like the sight of the horrible motion of a mass of maggots in their carrion bed." On Gellner's monism versus Geertz's pluralism as exemplified in the issue of segmentary tribal structure in North Africa, see Lawrence Rosen, *The Culture of Islam: Changing Aspects of Contemporary Muslim Life*

(Chicago: University of Chicago Press, 2002), 42–43. See generally, Roland Hall, "Monism and Pluralism," in *The Encyclopedia of Philosophy,* vol. 5, ed. Paul Edwards (New York: Macmillan, 1967), 363–65.

5. George Kateb, "Can Cultures Be Judged? Two Defenses of Cultural Pluralism in Isaiah Berlin's Work," *Social Research* 66, no. 4 (1999): 1009–38, at 1012. Geertz uses the term "systems," which was also the title (together with "careers") of the core graduate course he helped to design during his years at Chicago, in numerous of his publications. See, for example, Clifford Geertz, "Religion as a Cultural System" and "Ideology as a Cultural System," in his *The Interpretation of Cultures* (New York: Basic Books, 1973), 87–125, 193–233; "Common Sense as a Cultural System" and "Art as a Cultural System," in his *Local Knowledge: Further Essays in Interpretive Anthropology* (New York: Basic Books, 1983), 74–120. On this period of his career at Chicago, see his "An Inconstant Profession: The Anthropological Life in Interesting Times," in *Annual Review of Anthropology* (Palo Alto, CA: Annual Reviews, 2002), 1–19, at 11–12; and *After the Fact: Two Countries, Four Decades, One Anthropologist* (Cambridge: Harvard University Press, 1995), 110–15.

6. This latter is said in reference to the debate over the meaning of Captain Cook's presence to the Hawaiians, a debate in which Geertz favors Sahlins's treatment over that of Obeyesekere: "I perhaps should at this point come clean and say that, for my part, I find Sahlins, the structuralist glitter surrounding his analyses aside, markedly the more persuasive. His descriptions are more circumstantial, his portrayal of both the Hawaiians and the British more deeply penetrating, and his grasp of the moral and political issues involved surer, less prey to the confusing noises of the confused present" (AL, 106). Compare Geertz's criteria of interpretation with those of Michael Walzer, *Interpretation and Social Criticism* (Cambridge: Harvard University Press, 1987), 30: "The best reading [of a poem] is not different in kind, but in quality, from the other readings: it illuminates the poem in a more powerful and persuasive way. Perhaps the best reading is a new reading, seizing upon some previously misunderstood symbol or trope and re-explaining the entire poem. The case is the same with moral interpretation: it will sometimes confirm and sometimes challenge received opinion."

7. In the field of literature, for example, see E. D. Hirsch Jr., *Validity in Interpretation* (New Haven: Yale University Press, 1967); and *The Aims of Interpretation* (Chicago: University of Chicago Press, 1976).

8. See Kateb, "Can Cultures Be Judged?" at 1011, 1016–18, and 1021. Stressing the relation of incommensurability to the comparativist project Geertz says: "Santayana's famous dictum, that one compares only when one is unable to get at the heart of the matter, is the precise reverse of the truth; it is through comparison, and of incomparables, that whatever heart we can actually get to is reached," *Local Knowledge,* 233.

9. Clifford Geertz, "The Visit: Review of Cai Hua, 'A Society without Fathers or Husbands: The Na of China,'" *New York Review of Books,* October 18, 2001, 29. Geertz goes on to say: "There is nothing, or almost nothing, of individual feelings and personal judgments, of hopes, fears, dissents, and resistances, of fantasy, remorse, pride, humor, loss, or disappointment. The question that in the end we most want answered and the one most insistently raised by the very circumstantiality of Hua's ethnography—'What is it like to be a Na?'—goes largely unattended. We are left with a compact, well-arranged world of rules, institutions, customs, and practices: a 'kinship system.' Can this be enough? 'Na-ness' as a form-of-life, a way-of-being-in-the-world, is, whatever it is, a much wider, more ragged, unsettled, less articulated, and less articulable thing. It is a mood and an atmosphere, a

suffusing gloss on things, and it is hard to describe or systematize, impossible to contain in summary categories."

10. Thus anti-relativism does not, for Geertz, mean treating any practice as acceptable: "The objection to anti-relativism is not that it rejects an it's-all-how-you-look-at-it approach to knowledge or a when-in-Rome approach to morality, but that it imagines that they can only be defeated by placing morality beyond culture and knowledge beyond both" (AL, 65). George Kateb says that for Berlin "the aesthetic observer must turn his back on the claims of morality and truth or resist their temptations; they are aesthetically irrelevant" ("Can Cultures Be Judged?" 1021). "Judging and ranking cultures by the extent to which they avoid or reduce injustice and untruth entangles us, Berlin seems to think, in indifference to creativity and hence to perils to the human stature" (ibid., 1037). Berlin's distaste for pursuing the untidiness of much of social life is well captured by Adam Gopnik when he writes: "Berlin lifts the curtain, peeks at the irrational, and then quickly closes it again, with a reassuring bow to his audience. It is squalid in there, but, fortunately, not too squalid to bear" ("The Porcupine: A Pilgrimage to Popper," *The New Yorker,* April 1, 2002, 88–93).

11. "To recognize the moral tension, the ethical ambiguity, implicit in the encounter of anthropologist and informant, and to still be able to dissipate it through one's actions and one's attitudes, is what encounter demands of both parties if it is to be authentic, if it is to actually happen" (AL, 37).

12. The phrase is from Kateb, "Can Cultures Be Judged?" 1020.

13. Walzer, *Interpretation and Social Criticism,* 23 (original italics).

14. Ibid., 22.

15. Yr Hen Gyrys O Ial, *The Red Book of Hergest,* 1397, quoted in Tristan Jones, *Adrift* (Dobbs Ferry, NY: Sheridan House, 1992).

16. Speaking about cultural diversity, Geertz writes: "My purpose is to suggest that we have come to such a point in the moral history of the world (a history itself of course anything but moral) that we are obliged to think about such diversity rather differently than we had been used to thinking about it. If it is getting to be the case that rather than being sorted into framed units, social spaces whose edges are unfixed, irregular, and difficult to locate, the question of how to deal with the puzzles of judgment to which such disparities give rise takes on a rather different aspect. Confronting landscapes and still life is one thing; panoramas and collages quite another" (AL, 85).

17. Clifford Geertz, *Works and Lives: The Anthropologist as Author* (Stanford: Stanford University Press, 1988), 113.

18. This position can also lead to certain misunderstandings about Geertz's position. For example, in one interview Geertz, pressed by the reporter, was reluctant to condemn female genital mutilation. This seemed to the interviewer to be an example of relativism, the refusing to take a position on the matter altogether, whereas it would be more accurate to see it as Geertz's refusal to pontificate as an anthropologist, emphasizing instead our need to know as much as possible about the context of the practice and then reach whatever judgments we may wish to reach separately (David Berreby, "Unabsolute Truths: Clifford Geertz," *New York Times Magazine,* April 9, 1995, 44–47). A more egregious example is Paul Rabinow's accusation that Geertz has no politics at all, or Vincent Crapanzano's charges of Geertzian "self-subversion." For Geertz's response, see his *Works and Lives,* 91–101. For an assessment of both commentators as exhibiting "[n]eurotic offendability together with a sort of childish lashing out" see Fred Inglis, *Clifford Geertz: Culture, Custom and Ethics* (Cambridge: Polity Press, 2000), 153–55. Each of these writers makes the mistake

of confuting what Geertz thinks we can (and realistically ought to) say as anthropologists with what we may be called upon to address as individuals.

19. It may be worth asking whether Heisenberg himself was applying his indeterminacy principle to his own moral acts. Neither in Michael Frayn's play *Copenhagen* nor in the discussions occasioned by it have I noted any indication of this possibility. It might, however, account for some of Heisenberg's action during the war. You cannot pursue a line of inquiry about the "pure" theory of atomic fission knowing it might result in an atomic bomb and, at the same time, take a stance of moral opposition to it; you can only do one at a time, seeing different things through each focus, knowing that within each vantage there must be a natural uncertainty. The advantage of moving back and forth between two such perspectives may have been that contradictions, even opposites, can appear, whether in physics or morality, as "natural" equivalents capable of producing equally valuable, yet equally uncertain, results. The analogies to moral thinking in the human sciences are intriguing.

20. Geertz thus quotes: "as a bar to . . . moral presumptuousness . . . what Jakob Burkhardt . . . said in 1860 about the dubious business of judging peoples: 'It may be possible to indicate many contrasts and shades of difference among different nations, but to strike the balance of the whole is not given to human insight. The ultimate truth with respect to the character, the conscience, and the guilt of a people remains for ever a secret; if only for the reason that its defects have another side, where they reappear as peculiarities or even as virtues. We must leave those who find pleasure in passing sweeping censures on whole nations, to do so as they like. The people of Europe can maltreat, but happily not judge one another. A great nation, interwoven in its civilization, its achievements, and its fortunes with the whole life of the modern world, can afford to ignore both its advocates and its accusers. It lives on with or without the approval of theorists' " (*The Civilization of the Renaissance of Italy* [New York: Modern Library, 1954], 318); quoted in Geertz, "Afterword: The Politics of Meaning," in *Culture and Politics in Indonesia,* ed. Claire Holt (Ithaca: Cornell University Press, 1972), 319–35, at 335.

21. Hilary Mantel, "Naipaul's Book of the World," *New York Review of Books,* October 24, 2002, 10–12, at 10.

22. Pauline Kael, *I Lost It at the Movies* (1965), quoted in Rosalie Maggio, compiler, *The Beacon Book of Quotations by Women* (Boston: Beacon Press, 1992), 178.

23. Geertz has at times opposed the anthropology association taking positions on political matters. It seems to him to smack of the old Soviet Academy of Sciences model, since (as we saw at the time of resolutions surrounding anthropological research and the Vietnam War) there was a serious temptation to read certain people out of the profession on the basis of one's position on the war dressed up as a particular form of action required in dealing with the peoples affected.

24. See, for example, Clifford Geertz, *Islam Observed: Religious Development in Morocco and Indonesia* (New Haven: Yale University Press, 1968), 98–117. For his most explicit assessment of developing nations and the criteria for appraising them, see Clifford Geertz, "The Judging of Nations: Some Comments on the Assessment of Regimes in the New States," *Archives européenes de sociologie/European Journal of Sociology* 18 (1977): 245–61.

25. Geertz also turned down an appointment at the Institute for Advanced Study when it was first offered in the late 1960s because universities like Chicago (where students had taken over the administration building) were in such turmoil over the Vietnam War. Geertz felt an obligation not to abandon the university at a time when everything appeared to be

politicized around that single event. That others took as political conservatism his refusal to let an issue of the moment lead to drastic repercussions for the institutions of higher education should more accurately be seen as concern that institutional alterations based on momentary events could be vastly destructive and lead to pressures for political conformity that universities above all should resist. His views as a person were very clear as concerned the war. What he rejected was not only the threat of political pressures within the academy; he resisted the idea that people should be able to claim political believability as anthropologists that could not be sustained on independent intellectual grounds.

REFERENCE

Geertz, Clifford. 2000. *Available Light: Anthropological Reflections on Philosophical Topics*. Princeton: Princeton University Press.

Celebrating Geertzian Interpretivism

CLIFF GEERTZ (ADVERTENTLY OR INADVERTENTLY) helped rescue me and my like-minded psychologist friends from the long, cold winter of anti-mentalism that had long ago stricken our beleaguered field of psychology. That's what I want to talk about, and I do so with gratitude.

In my own case, indeed the rescue extended even beyond psychology, for more latterly I have been increasingly preoccupied with psychological and cultural issues in law and jurisprudence. Cliff's emphasis on the role of meaning-making in the law has been as important to me in the study of the law as it had been when, earlier, we were all in the midst of the Cognitive Revolution which, by the way, is now in the process of being "culturalized"! So bravo to his 1960s Storrs Lectures at the Yale Law School, of which more presently, and of which you'll find echoes in a recent book of mine and Tony Amsterdam.[1]

So what was this Geertzian influence? Let me go back to the beginnings, to the 1960s. Cliff tells an intriguing tale about how, during those early years of his at Chicago, he joined forces with "restless" colleagues there "to redefine the ethnographical enterprise whole and entire."[2] The effort, as he tells it, "consisted in placing the systematic study of meaning at the very center of research and analysis to make of anthropology, or anyway cultural psychology, a hermeneutical discipline." And the "move toward meaning," indeed "proved a proper revolution: sweeping, durable, turbulent, and consequential," to use his words again, a quarter century later.[3]

I'm sure that none of that Chicago gang had it in mind to rescue psychologist from psychology's chilling, objectivist self-made plight. They were fielding enough flak from their fellow anthropologists to have little time for rescue operations elsewhere. Yet, for all that, the new meaning-centered "interpretivism" in cultural anthropology began having its "unsetting" effects on psychologists very early on. I must say a word about the why and wherefore of these effects.

You see, at its start, psychology had been torn by two conflicting views about how to understand the human condition—through a day view or a night view, to translate founding-father Gustave Fechner's Tagesansicht and Nachtansicht. The night view sought the idiosyncratic dramatic-historical patterns of human experience; the day view searched for content-free constants of experience that could be discerned in sensation, perception, memory—like Weber's law to the effect that a just noticeable difference in sensation, any sensation, was always a constant fraction of the sensation presently in force. Weber was our would-be Newton! Even as late as the turn of the century (at least in Europe) it was moot as to which approach had prevailed—the scientific Naturwissenshaftlich way of the hard sciences or the humanistic interpretivist way of the Geisteswissenschaften. But by the time my generation arrived on the scene, just as the Second World War was starting—the natural-science approach had been long, loudly, and officially declared the winner, at least on our shores. And since, at least in America, we love converting the outcomes of uncertain struggles into zero-sum form, interpretivism had been declared dead and gone. Yes, there were still obscure pockets where the insights of the novelist or dramatist were provisionally acceptable, but only faute de mieux until "real" psychology could clean up the mess. Interpretivism was methodological weakness or just plain slovenliness: forgivable if provisional as with a Gordon Allport; unforgivable if insistent, as with psychoanalysis. We all read Freud anyway and I recall I. A. Richards's lectures on literary interpretation with relived delight, even getting a few of my fellow graduate students to trek next door to Sever Hall with me, sneaking across a corner of the Harvard Yard to get a breath of humanist air.

When it came to research, though, we all went strictly kosher, or at least we kept our yarmulkes well pinned on! If I wanted to explore anything that sounded "cultural," I made it a point to use the most psychophysically exquisite cover I could find—as with the so-called New Look in perception where, with the most meticulous controls going, I showed that kids overestimated the sizes of coins proportionately to their value, the more so for poor kids than better-off ones. Or I used the soon-to-be-famous Harvard tachistoscope to demonstrate that a black four-of-clubs playing card took only 200 milliseconds to recognize visually, where a red one took 800 milliseconds of exposure. The word "culture" does not appear in the papers reporting those results, nor does the term "meaning." We'd already learned by then how to avoid quarrels with psychology journal referees! Even Gordon Allport got raised hackles at the idea (once mooted metaphorically by Kroeber at a Harvard seminar he guest-conducted) that mind might be the subjective side culture!

You can well understand that what Cliff and his early 1960s Chicago friends were proposing was (at least for a psychologist) far more radical than they may have realized. We listened with rather concealed interest. Then Cliff's ethnographic field studies began appearing—I recall particularly the Balinese Cockfight—demonstrating what you could do by keeping your eye firmly on the meaning-making process. And what struck me at the time was that meaning-making so often demanded storytelling, narrative for its realization—whatever that was psychologically. Oddly, to this day I wonder why Cliff doesn't get more explicit about the place of narrative in meaning-making, and, for that matter, in culture-forming generally. Perhaps he's still worried about the hard-nosed colleagues who like to attack him. Better to keep your literary background from showing too plainly in public! For all that, I'm very touched by the following rather covert and quite out-of-the-blue passage that ends the Preface to Cliff's 1988 *Works and Lives: The Anthropologist as Author:* "Finally, in lieu of a dedication, which would be presumptuous, I would like merely to mention the name of the man, nowhere cited in the body of the text, who has had no direct connection to it or me, but whose works has served as its governing inspiration at almost every point: Kenneth Burke."

For those not acquainted with Burke, his 1924 *The Grammar of Motives,* with its stunning concept of "dramatism" is the birthplace of American literary consciousness about the role of narrative in culturally shaped meaning-making. For Burke, narrative is our mode for making sense of breaches in our culturally canonical expectations. And if you can find no narrative, you are lost—like that poor Balinese Regreg in the first of Cliff's Storrs Lectures, unable to accept the local narrative resolutions of his overturned expectancies, ones that might conventionalize his plight as a deserted husband. He finally goes out of his mind.[4]

Finally, to the law. I happen to believe that Cliff's Storrs Lectures of thirty years ago may be his greatest contribution to intellectual life beyond anthropology. They reverberate in the legal academy today as never before, as exemplified, say, in Paul Kahn's recent book.[5] For interpretation is, of course, the heart of law. Legal interpretation, we now know more clearly, is the assigning of factual accounts, usually in story form, to normative standards in the law that specify what's a violation, what isn't. But the normative standards specified in the law must be congruent with, in some obvious way derivable from the norms of the culture. Fact itself can never be independent of law—"our vision and our verdicts ratify one another," he says. And law itself cannot transcend the meaning-ways of culture. As Kahn puts it, "Law must rule the imagination before it can rule the state."[6]

Cliff's masterly demonstration in his Storrs Lecture of this fact-law-culture interdependence in Islamic *haqq* law (presumably based on "truth"), Indic dharma law (presumably on criteria of "duty"), and in Malay-Polynesia *adat* law (on standards of "custom") has had a powerful impact. It has not led so much to reform movements (the lawyer's usual hyperactive response to new ideas), but rather to consciousness-raising about the inherent dangers and benefits in any system of law, including our own.

Let me sum up Cliff's contribution in his own words: "The interpretive study of culture represents an attempt to come to terms with the diversity of the ways human beings construct their lives in the act of leading them."[7] And, to return to the beginning, it was his dedicated effort to come to terms with that credo that inspired not only anthropologists but also those dissident psychologists unhappy with their discipline's proclaimed devotion to the one-way street of positivist science.

Thank you, Cliff. You once wrote me, after you'd read my 1990 book, *Acts of Meaning*,[8] "We really are doing the same thing, only you call it psychology, because you got your license there, and I call it anthropology, because that's where I got mine." I too am convinced that you can't do either anthropology or psychology without coming to terms with meaning and the contexts in which it is made. And I think that truth makes the distinction between them not so much useless, but misleading. We're all in the same boat now, never mind the seas aren't quite yet charted!

NOTES

1. Anthony G. Amsterdam and Jerome Bruner, *Minding the Law* (Cambridge: Harvard University Press, 2000).

2. Clifford Geertz, *After the Fact: Two Countries, Four Decades, One Anthropologist* (Cambridge: Harvard University Press 1995), 114.

3. Geertz, *After the Fact,* 114–15.

4. See Clifford Geertz, "Local Knowledge: Fact and Law in Comparative Perspective," chapter 8 in his *Local Knowledge: Further Essays in Interpretive Anthropology*, 3rd ed. (New York: Basic Books, 2000).

5. See, for example, the acclaimed *The Cultural Study of Law: Reconstructing Legal Scholarship,* by Yale law professor Paul W. Kahn (Chicago: University of Chicago Press, 1999).

6. Kahn, *Cultural Study,* 83.

7. Geertz, *Local Knowledge,* 16.

8. Jerome Bruner, *Acts of Meaning* (Cambridge: Harvard University Press, 1990).

Coded Communications
Symbolic Psychological Anthropology

A T THE TOP OF MY LIST of books that will never be written is
Principia Semiotica by Clifford Geertz. The book jacket says, "This
book summarizes concisely all that is known about human symbolic systems. A few simple axioms are shown to generate all cultural variations
past and present, actual and possible, in just ten pages of text. The de-
ductive algorithm may be difficult for lay readers to understand, but the
book comes with a compact disk that you can put into your computer
to design your own symbolic system or simulate those of the Amazon or
Himalayas. This work represents a new anthropological science eclips-
ing all previous efforts that were based on the crude approximations of
ethnography—thus launching the discipline of anthropology as a science
equivalent to particle physics and molecular genetics."

It should be no surprise that Clifford Geertz never wrote this book,
but there was a time in the 1970s when the rumor went around that
something like it was in the works, that Geertz was going to unveil his
Theory in a formal exposition that would revolutionize anthropological
thought and research. It is now clear that Cliff has always been extremely
allergic to this kind of theorizing (Geertz 2000, 3–20) and that he developed and pursued an alternative conception of cultural anthropology that
has affected the thinking of a wide circle of those inside and outside the
discipline, to our great benefit.

Cliff and I were students together in the Harvard Department of Social Relations during the early 1950s. He was three years ahead of me,
but we breathed the same air, with its aroma of scientism, which I found
intoxicating and he found distasteful—a reaction on his part already formulated in terms of phenomenology and informed by humanistic studies.
He already had the goal of finding a place for cultural anthropology free
of scientistic pretensions, that is, the formalizations of theory and method
that simplify social and cultural realities in imitation of the natural sciences. Our views were far apart on this issue.

Cliff and I overlapped again, this time on the faculty of the University

of Chicago, from 1960 to 1970, where we both participated from its beginning in the Committee for the Comparative Study of New Nations.
I spent a large part of that decade studying at the Chicago Institute for
Psychoanalysis where, in contrast to anthropologists whose psychoanalytic training convinced them of Freudian universals—"pre-cultural" and
"extra-cultural" aspects of the human psyche—I moved in the opposite
direction, toward an appreciation of the clinical phenomenology of psychoanalysis rather than its grand theory. A major reason for this change
was the influence of one of my teachers at the Institute, Heinz Kohut,
who appears in Cliff's "Thick Description" as the author of the distinction between "experience-near" and "experience-distant" concepts (Kohut 1971). Kohut saw clinical psychoanalysis as an exercise in "empathic
understanding," and of course ethnography is based on empathic understanding too. In contrast to the approach of other Freudians faced with
cultural phenomena, Kohut advocated working carefully from the surface available to observation to the depths of theoretical inference and
reconstruction (LeVine 1992). He was teaching this psychoanalytic phenomenology during the 1960s but only gradually brought it out in print
for fear of appearing too radical within the orthodox world of the American Psychoanalytic Association.

This was of course the same time that Cliff was publishing the papers
collected in *The Interpretation of Cultures* (1973), which formulated the
basic terms of his symbolic action theory. This theory, together with Victor Turner's (1967) work on ritual and Bob Levy's (1973) ethnopsychol-
ogy, eventually convinced me that some combination of Geertz's symbolic action approach and Kohut's self psychology could lead to the most
promising "person-centered ethnography," as I called it, for research in
psychological anthropology (LeVine 1982). In the present context, however, I want to acknowledge the foundational importance of the culture
concept as Cliff revitalized it in the 1960s and 1970s. It is indispensable
for psychological anthropology, and I shall illustrate briefly why I think so.

When I talk about Geertzian symbolic action theory I mean first of all
the premise that all communicative action is coded, that is, it has reference to a shared symbolic code, like the wink that Cliff made famous—a
code that is local and complex rather than universal and simple—and can
require lengthy translation and explication. Communication is the very
center of what we investigate in psychological anthropology, as Gregory
Bateson taught us long ago; the understanding that it is always coded
in terms that draw their meanings from the history, values, and conceptions of a community is fundamental to our research. Second, by symbolic

action theory I mean the metaphor of a cultural model that combines normative and descriptive dimensions and operates like computer software, selectively actualizing human potentials for cognition, emotion, motivation, and action. This view can breathe new life into the dullest corners of human existence.

Take childcare, for example. What could be more mundane, routine, and repetitive? Some think it should be understood simply in terms of strategic formulas for allocating the time and energy of mothers and maintaining the caloric intake of their offspring—as biologists analyze parental care in other vertebrate species (Wilson 1975). Looked at in terms of symbolic action, however, childcare in humans is freighted with moral ideology and emotion, particularly when examined in comparative and historical perspective. These cultural meanings are presumed by, embedded in, and signaled by the communicative actions of parents and others interacting with the child, drawing on population-specific codes of speech and conduct. Rick Shweder (Shweder et al. 1997), Sara Harkness (Harkness and Super 1996) and I, and our colleagues and students, make nuisances of ourselves among psychologists by pointing this out with better and better evidence. We have made some progress in convincing child development researchers.

Yet cultural models of human parental care cannot simply be reduced to cultural values any more than they can be validly reduced to rational strategies. I have argued, following Geertz, that we have to see them as susceptible to both semiotic and utilitarian analyses, with the former identifying the moral directions and conventional norms of childcare practices, while the latter reveal the pragmatic strategies and logistical tactics involved (LeVine et al. 1994). Parent-child communication is culturally coded but its canonical forms in a particular community have their own logic and responsiveness to environmental pressures. The Geertzian perspective enables us to keep these two aspects in focus.

Thus cultural analysis following Geertz is crucial in psychological anthropology, not only for the understanding of childhood environments but also in all other arenas of social communication. I thank him for taking it as his task from his student days onward to cut "culture" down to size, rejecting the omnibus concepts formulated by anthropologists from Edward B. Tylor (1871) to our teacher Clyde Kluckhohn (Kroeber and Kluckhohn, 1952), in favor of an ideational concept with "a determinate application, a definite sense and a specified use" (Geertz 2000, 13); his success in this endeavor has not only deepened our insights into the central subject of the discipline but also given us a tool for ethnographic investigation and interpretation.

But what of the arguments made by some psychological anthropologists (Ewing 1992; Strauss and Quinn 1997, 13–20) that Geertz denies the importance of private mental contents, psychological processes and personal experience in favor of public communication, leaving us to guess at what his psychology consists of—or worse yet, leading us to assume he believes that anthropology or symbolic action theory can do without a psychology? I don't believe that Geertz has no psychology, partly because I know he pays attention to the literatures of psychology and psychoanalysis and partly because I feel certain that he agrees with psychological anthropologists that every concept of culture makes psychological assumptions. So I shall end by asking him to join us in considering the psychology of culture, as Sapir called it, and make public his views about this difficult but fundamental subject.

REFERENCES

Ewing, Katherine. 1992. Is Psychoanalysis Relevant for Anthropology? In *New Directions in Psychological Anthropology,* ed. Theodore Schwartz, Geoffrey White, and Catherine Lutz. New York: Cambridge University Press.

Geertz, Clifford. 1973. *The Interpretation of Cultures.* New York: Free Press.

———. 2000. *Available Light: Anthropological Reflections on Philosophical Topics.* Princeton: Princeton University Press.

Harkness, Sara, and Charles Super, eds. 1996. *Parents' Cultural Belief Systems.* New York: Guilford Press.

Kohut, Heinz. 1971. *The Analysis of the Self.* New York: International Universities Press.

Kroeber, Alfred L., and Clyde Kluckhohn. 1952. Culture: A Critical Review of Concepts and Definitions. *Papers of the Peabody Museum of Archaeology and Ethnology* 47, no. 1. Cambridge, MA: Peabody Museum.

LeVine, Robert A. 1982. *Culture, Behavior and Personality,* 2nd. ed. New York: Aldine Publishing.

———. 1992. The Self in an African Culture. In *Psychoanalytic Anthropology after Freud: Essays Marking the Fiftieth Anniversary of Freud's Death,* ed. D. H. Spain. New York: Psyche Press.

LeVine, Robert A., S. Dixon, S. E. LeVine, A. Richman, P. H. Leiderman, C. Keefer, and T. B. Brazelton. 1994. *Child Care and Culture: Lessons from Africa.* New York: Cambridge University Press.

Levy, Robert I. 1973. *Tahitians.* Chicago: University of Chicago Press.

Shweder, Richard A., J. Goodnow, G. Hatano, R. A. LeVine, H. Markus, and P. Miller. 1997. *The Cultural Psychology of Development.* In *The Handbook of Child Psychology,* vol. 1, ed. William Damon. New York: Wiley.

Strauss, Claudia, and Naomi Quinn. 1997. *A Cognitive Theory of Cultural Meaning.* New York: Cambridge University Press.

Turner, Victor W. 1967. *The Forest of Symbols.* Ithaca: Cornell University Press.

Tylor, Edward B. 1871. *Primitive Culture.* London: John Murray.

Wilson, Edward O. 1975. *Sociobiology.* Cambridge: Harvard University Press.

Geertz's Style
A Moral Matter

> Like Bismarck's sausages, [I] have seen [it] made.
>
> Clifford Geertz, *Available Light*

M Y TITLE'S LEADING MOTIVE stems from Cliff's "Art as a Cultural System"—with its studiously strange comparison: veering from colloquially sculpted body slashes (Yoruba) and declamatory color-shapes (Abelard); to Quattrocento painting (that's Italian) as a gauging (Piero della Francesca), a preaching (Fra Angelico), and a dancing (Botticelli); to radically unvisual performance art: Moroccan intersections of Qur'anic memorization, Arabic media, and festive poetizing. In this third sort of world, Geertz suggests, verbal style is a moral matter. Now Cliff is no Muslim—nor anything else recognizably doctrinal (judging from *After the Fact* and "Passage and Accident"). So, how can his written "style" (think of it as a "thinking") be a moral matter, a moral act even?

(I'm thinking here of "Thinking as a Moral Act," Cliff's 1968 *Antioch Review* essay on mutual ironies pervading fieldwork encounters and inequalities. That fine piece missed two previous boats of collection. Although prior to "Thick Description," it was not found [even in translation] in *The Interpretation of Cultures;* although unfootnotedly approachable [like "Blurred Genres," another *Antioch Review* original], it lacked in *Local Knowledge.* That it didn't make the cut sooner has a nice consequence [intended or un-]. *Available Light,* erring, if it errs, on the side of erudition, includes an un-up-to-date item less taxing than now-neighboring pieces, e.g., "Anti Anti-Relativism"—that prickly disquisition first delivered to the AAA in 1981, also now long-ago. But I digress.)

To resume: Can an offbeat, various, and assertively liberal corpus help impel—citing the final phrase of *Available Light*'s last paragraph that sports just one proper name: E. M. Forster (Two Cheers!!)—"the moral obligation to hope?" Did somebody say "liberal"? Yes, indeed; Cliff confesses as much, albeit in that flickeringly indirect way of his:

> Those who would therefore, promote the causes for which these names, and others more nearly contemporary—Dewey, Camus, Berlin ["Isaiah," this

Tin-Pan Alley buff reminds himself], Kuron, Taylor—in their various ways variably stand (for "liberalism," too, is neither compact nor homogeneous, and it is certainly unfinished) need to recognize its culturally specific origin and its culturally specific character. (Geertz, *Available Light*, 2000 [hereafter AL], 259)

Like *The Religion of Java* and anything else "cultural" ("The Balinese Village," say), each subject-interpreted varies, indeed variably varies. Whatever is "gotten at" (as Geertz says) varies (e.g., "The Abangan Variant")—including variable liberalism, such as Cliff's own (and mine). A variant (Boasian) name for all this is "disaggregation"—an interpretive tactic enacting philosophical commitment to ironic certainties of cultures' ever-translated unfinishedness. But that's another essay.[1]

Let me, then, repeat (varyingly) a leading-motive of this one. Does Cliff's more-than-mere rhetoric (think of rhetoric as thinking-style) do something? Are his exactingly shaggy sentences—fashioned into peculiarly persuasive juxtapositions, in essays re-collected, sometimes, non-chronologically—"agentive" (to recall Kenneth Burke)?

Or recall again those Moroccan Muslims in *Local Knowledge* whose everyday speech-acts (agonistic "speech-actings," I'd say) strike Cliff as efficacious, or nearly. Even their idle, catch-as-catch-can conversations— "a head-on collision of curses, promises, lies, excuses, pleading, commands, proverbs, arguments, analogies, quotations, threats, evasion, flatteries . . . gives to rhetoric a directly coercive force; (*'andu klam*), "he has words, speech, maxims, eloquence," means also, and not just metaphorically, "he has power, influence, weight, authority" (Geertz, *Local Knowledge*, 1983 [hereafter LK], 114). Is there a kind of *'andu klam* (pardon my Arabic; my tin-ear for it traces to loanwords in Indonesian)—a virtuoso forcefulness—to Cliff's own eloquence, earthiness, and maxims (including maxims about *'andu klam*)? Could be; I've a hunch there is; one might, sure 'nuff, suppose so.

To catch-as-catch-can the "how" of Cliff's corpus—the voice of his theory composed (like certain poetry) out of voices encountered—I'm trying here to emulate his "moral-matter" itself. Trying conspicuously, and surely flubbing. Because Geertz's style is truly difficult—in George Steiner's precise sense; and pastiche is easier (although in its precise operatic sense, less so than proverbially falling off the proverbial log). I'll try to get less pastichey (and patchy) later, but first a few random salutes to Geertzwerk—my name for the beast.[2]

GEERTZWERK: spanning half a century, bridging two millennia, crafting countless comparisons, in prose both manifold and singular. Open any Geertzwerk anywhere—about Java, about Morocco, about Bali (e.g., *Bali: Interprétation d'une culture,* with "Deep Play" rendered "jeu d'enfer" [that's "deep"!]); or about all three ("Muslims, Hindus, and one disguised as the other," in Cliff's loving quip on Javanese)—and it's still Geertz: one radically UNUNIFORM anthropology. The achingly plural style is nevertheless culturally (in Cliff's sense) American, a variant of our philosophical "catalogue rhetoric"—or so I have intimated elsewhere (Boon 1999). Yes, list-laden vernacular discursivity is Cliff's "special somewhere" (not a neutral nowhere)—his being here-and-there in open (liberal) conversation with cultures everywhere, wondering how "people with differences can live among one another with some degree of comity" (AL, 260).[3]

Back in 1982, I impishly designated Cliff anthropology's equivalent of "James, both William and Henry"; ensuing years have not dissuaded me.[4] Hardly stagnant, his signature generalization-eschewing grows ever more caveated, colloquial, caustic, scatter-shot—always courageous, and as corrosive as it is consoling: quite suited to our world, I'd say. A William James component is now patent in "The Pinch of Destiny"; to appreciate Geertz's Henry James side, I recommend parsing such "sentences" as:

> Rather than conceiving of a legal system, our own or any other, as divided between trouble over what is right and trouble over what is so (to use Llewellyn's piquant formulation, if only because it has been so influential among anthropologists) and of "juristic technique," our own or any other, as a matter of squaring ethical decisions responding to the what is right sort with empirical determinations responding to the what is so sort, it would seem better—more "realistic," if I may say so—to see such systems as describing the world and what goes on in it in explicitly judgmatical terms and such "technique" as an organized effort to make the description [PAUSE . . .] correct. (LK, 174)

What reader negotiating this prosey maze could ever anticipate it's concluding word? Perhaps an aficionado of James (Henry). The confabulation just delivered graces Cliff's unremittingly circumstantial inquiry into "law and fact" (contrasting (Islamic/Hindu/Christian/"secular"/etc.). That study reads at moments like late-James: runaway nuance of affect and mood; yet it also offers crisp aphorisms such as Larry Rosen's paper culled from Cliff's verbal hothouse of "comparative perspective."

Yes, didactic aspects remain key even in their relative abatement, as later-Geertzwerk forswears theoretic synthesis acerbically yet also doubts easy declarations of absolute free-play or cozy proclamations of post-theoreticism's triumph. Cliff perhaps remains not unopen (pardon my litotes) to relative systematishness, provided we recognize its contingent ("unfinished") quality. And regarding that unfinishedness he is still liable to become, rarely, didactic, preachy even. (Recall the close of *After the Fact,* whose prose abruptly, and helpfully, halts to explain, figurative pointer in hand, punning undercurrents of its title. You'd almost suspect some editor had requested this, and Cliff had, perhaps grudgingly, obliged.)

Sermons I myself have published elsewhere, designate this family of style "relative (not absolute) relativism"; I somewhat prefer "relative relativism" to "anti anti-relativism" but only for the nonce. Either formulation (and they are close relatives) resists overblown theorizing (or anti-theorizing)—too intent on apotheosizing this or that, or demonizing that or this. [5]

One shining moment of "relative relativizing" is Cliff's recent allusion to four centuries of critical consciousness (Montaigne through Foucault, say), with a provocative twist and thrust I'd characterize as: Neither Bentham, nor Foucault; perhaps Montaigne with Weber. In case you missed it, I quote:

> If advances in the technical, fine-tuning control of social life (Bentham's dream, Foucault's nightmare) is what you are after, then universality talk is, I guess, the talk to talk. If you are after refinements in our ability to live lives that make some sense to us and of which we can on balance approve (Montaigne's skeptical hope, Weber's desperate one)—moral skills, not manipulative ones—then something less vaulting would seem to be called for.

That's *Available Light,* page 139, for those of us taking notes; and it provides my paper's second leading motive.

"Something less vaulting" (yet uncommonly learned!)—may just be what Cliff's cross-cultural writing has always been writing-about. What does ethnographer-Geertz do (practice): he writes-about, unmanipulatively. Not just *écrire,* but *décrire* (*écrire de* . . . right, Natalie?). Call it description, and call it thick. Yet, to paraphrase Lady Chatterley's gamekeeper (old what's-his-name, besides "Sir John"), "You have to ta'e the thick with the thin!" And Cliff has addressed (sometimes thinly) superficial play (versus deep) as well—including his sole reference to Doris Day and Montgomery Clift in *The Religion of Java* (page 307). I broached such thick/thin dilemmas as spiritedly as I dared (*berani*) in "Showbiz as a

Cross-Cultural System" published in *Cultural Anthropology,* anno 2000. All of you please read that ardent effort (and buy the book [Boon, 1999] to which it serves as *boutade,* aftermath, or sign-off). I hoped to *show* why Geertz's writing-about (*décrire*) requires rereading (*relire*). Indeed *décrire-pour-relire* is (for me, anyway) his *Beruf.*[6]

Cliff himself, of course, remains a reading-ethnographer, diversely educated you might say; and it was ever so. Remember *The Religion of Java* (based on his 1955 dissertation "report," published with new framing devices in 1960, read by me in 1965 because of HIM [pointing to Jim Peacock], the first year of the paperback version, my copy of which I marked in red, as sophomores then were inclined to do (studious ones, anyway). On page 337, I might have underlined (but stupidly failed to):

> Perhaps Shaw's comment [for those taking notes, that's George Bernard
> Shaw, unreferenced and unindexed, in this book on *Java* (*try to sound like*
> *Ray Romano*)] that the only trouble with Christianity is that it has never
> been tried is applicable to religion generally; for certainly there is much
> rivalry and backbiting among the various sects and a universal intolerance
> on their part for Islam, often on the grounds of its intolerance. But it is
> nevertheless true that the syncretistic, tolerant, relativistic outlook toward
> religious belief fits well with the whole tenor of *prijaji* mysticism. (Geertz,
> *Religion of Java,* 1976 [hereafter RJ], 337)

That's from "The *Prijaji* Variant" (the courtlyfied civil-service gentry); the chapter is "Mysticism"—duly disaggregated by Cliff throughout; the topic is "religious relativism," and it is chokingly sad to re-experience these pages, given Indonesian history today.

Yes, Cliff's opening opus already began fashioning wildly well-read ethnography that nudged readers (or, this one anyway) to dip into stray sources: Shaw, even. Geertzwerk's digressive *décriture* (writing-about) began and remained dramatically trans-disciplinarian *and* eccentrically solo. The approach seems cultivated to be engaged both companionably and edgily—not to be standardized or methodized. Indeed, standardized methodology Cliff's corpus stands against.

Yet for all its "unmethodicalness," Geertzwerk manages to be "didactic enough" (as when "Thinking as a Moral Act" waddles [the verb is Forster's] belatedly into *Available Light*). His catch-as-catch-can craft cagily (and catchily) encourages novices to stay the course of learning to fathom, comparatively, the un-outlineable. Cliff's pedagogic devices include so-called native's point of view (a Jamesian notion) and paradoxical gauges of experience near/distant. The latter idea repackages "emic/etic"—itself too experience-distant sounding to capture the distinction "experience near/distance" in an experience-near fashion. The help-ful heuristic we cling to becomes fraught; crisp distinction melts away. Nor, by the way, does experience-near correspond to "native's point of view"; for example:

> The [Arabic] word for poetry, *s'ir,* means "knowledge," and though no Muslim would explicitly put it that way, it stands as a kind of secular coun-terpoise, a worldly footnote, to the Revelation itself.

Here, what may seem experience-near for implied readers is precisely how no Muslim would (per Muslim) put it. Yes, experience near/distant is as convo(invo?)luted as everything else in Cliff's interpretive turns, including "thick."

To reiterate: writing-about, rereadably, truly-tricky difficulties of hu-manity's agonistic conversation (call it translation) is Geertz's *Beruf.* That term was Luther's (among others); its nondogmatic adaptation was We-ber's (after prolonged etymological parsing!). No more Lutheran than he is Muslim, Cliff enacts, nevertheless, anthropology *als Beruf* (and *als 'andu klam!*)—a Weberian dimension implicit throughout his style. Whatever else a *Beruf* might be, it is a little like a religion: a moral act and a moral matter.[7]

Panically short on time, how might I frame Cliff's "life and work" (*l'homme et le style; l'homme est le style*) in a semi-systematisch way? Well, consider its tripartite modes:

1. The oscillatingly contrastive (entrepreneurship in Java/Bali; irriga-tion in Bali/Morocco; three cases of anything "as a cultural system" or even "as an anti-anti."

2. The unpanoptic *panorame:* spicy overviews, all pith and no abstrac-tion, less "march of time" than wayward shuffle. Here's one of hundreds:

> [Indonesia] is . . . the product of an incredible stream of warring mind-sets—Portuguese, Spanish, Dutch, Indian, Chinese, Hindu, Buddhist, Confucian, Muslim, Christian; Capitalist, Communist, Imperial Administrative—carried by means of those great world-historical agencies, long-distance commod-ity trade, religious missionization, and colonial exploitation, into a vast, thousand-island archipelago occupied mainly . . . by Malayo-Polynesians, speaking hundreds of languages, following hundreds of cults, and possessed of hundreds of moralities, laws, customs, and arts; hundreds of senses, sub-tly different or grossly, reasonably concordant or deeply opposed, of how life ought to go. (AL, 253)[8]

3. The exponentially local, framed performatively. Here's an intimate for-instance:

Usually this is a lamp-lit space before the house of some wedding giver or circumcision celebrant. The poet stands, erect as a tree [whether for wedding or circumcision!] in the center. . . . Behind him are two lines of sidewise dancing men, . . . heads swiveling as they shuffle a couple half-steps right, a couple left. He sings his poem, verse by verse, paced by the tambourines in a wailed metallic falsetto, the assistants join him for the refrain . . . only generally related to the text, while the dancing men ornament matters with sudden strange rhythmic howls. (LK, 112)

In sum, whether (1) oscillatingly, (2) unpanoptic-panoramically, or (3) local-performatively, *décrire-pour-relire* enacts intersensory condensations of time-over-space through "mots justes" that reverberate interpretive hunches and doubts.

Adjective-noun combos are Cliff's special knack ("rhythmic howls"); modulated, rather than merely mordant, wit his habit. An assonant prose-poetics deserves savoring; a few favorites: aVaiLable Light (note the un-howling rhythm and delicate ring, a silkier title than "anthropology's awkwardness" one key theme (AL, 248). With "aVaiLable Light" in ear, listen back earlier: "simplicity flees"; "hypothesis hedgehogs"; "fugitive truth"; "almost monotonous" (as in "Next to Sefrou, Manhattan is almost monotonous"); "jural mimesis"; "legal imminglement (I can think of no exacter a word)"; and come to think of it, "exacter a word" (LK, 32, 150, 18, 127).

Nor are Geertzy *mots* necessarily mellifluous: "poets as horses." Or, shifting cadences now, "bush Picasso," "noisy Debussy"— coined to convey how Westerners might ethnocentrically process African art and game-lan music. All this in a book whose conceivable titles were: *Colloquial Reason; Vernacular Wisdom; Vehicles of Meaning: Their Ethnography; Curves of Someone Else's Experience; At-Home "S'ir"*—none as catchy (and catch-can) as *LoKKal KNowledge,* which concept by the way Cliff defends, and ardently, on seven pages of *Available Light* (133–40).

Geertzwerk thus achieves sustained attention to human foibles of circumstance (that's "foibles of," not "Pomp and . . ."). Even when earlier studies assessed potentials of economic take-off (*Peddlers and Princes*) or envisioned nation-building solidarity (*The Religion of Java*), contradiction and contingency percolated through. Try opening, say, the latter to page 96, and read closely, closely, closely. Two print fonts—the smaller for field notes (slightly polished, and written-down some hours "after the fact," anyhow—check Cliff's afterword on "method" (sort of); the larger font for commentary and expert-sounding explanation (kind of). But the division of interpretive labor smudges; "natives" too are explaining, and "anthropologist" too is doubting, and vice versa, blurily. With space, I'd copy out the entire page to encourage you to read aloud—smaller print softer, and larger print, louder (or vice versa?)—to gauge how Cliff's twinned fonts of descriptive prose should sound. Short of that here's a flattened sample:

[*Softer?*] He said he is not a *dukun* but merely a *pitulung* (I have never heard this term applied except by a man to himself; for everyone else, this man was a *dukun*). I asked him what the difference was, and he said a *dukun* takes money, but a *pitulung* doesn't—just helps people out. He said he can't always cure people; sometimes he can and sometimes he can't. If he could say for certain, "I can cure you," there would be two gods. As it is, he just supplicates God. . . . although he admitted he said spells over three hen's eggs . . . , and accepted gifts from satisfied patients.

[*Louder?*] There are several factors clustering around the psychological relationship between the *dukun* and his patient which seem to account for the ambivalent attitude most people show toward *dukuns*. The first . . . the uncertain outcome of treatment. . . . The second, the degree the *dukun* may become involved in his patient's personal life. . . . And the last is the inherent ambiguity of the *dukun*'s power, trafficking as he does both with God and with devils—*ndukuni* ("to *dukun* someone") means both to cure a person of a disease and to sorcerize a person into having one. . . . The major alternative term for *dukun* is *tijang sepuh*, which means (in the respectful speech style) "parent."

As early as *The Religion of Java,* what at first blush looks caveated about "experience" (e.g., cure) becomes caveated about explanation as well. It's as though evidence and interpretation were already doing a do-si-do, as though circumstantial doubt were as salient as so-called knowledge. *Que,* indeed, *sais-je?*

Since 1960, the loud (didactic) and the soft (descriptive) in Cliff's corpus have often in a sense switched priorities; nothing, however, has been scotched; pedagogy too maintains a say, a voice. Engaged in reading and rereading Geertzwerk, I feel, today like yesterday, "obligated to hope" that its future include much more writing-about, hermeneutically looping hither and yon, perhaps addressing again the circumstantial opera of Max Weber. Yes, I love anticipating still further culminations (along with the Deweyan) of Clifford James Geertz's *inimitable* style, a moral matter enacted and . . . Unfinished . . . !

NOTES

The epigraph is from page 252, antecedents altered, with a fond wink.

≈

Let me take this endnote-occasion to thank everyone responsible for and involved in the wonderful AAA panel. My piece was devised in a performance-flavor I here try to preserve. In New Orleans I opened with an ad-libbed-admission that, unlike Rick Shweder, I would assuredly not be ignoring Cyrano's nose. Cliff's scintillating proximity made me especially glad for the burst of applause after I risked delivering one of his amazing phrasings "my way." I felt confident enough (but only just) that Cliff recognized my efforts as neither parody nor pastiche (except operatically), but rather as a "pragmatic instantiation." (I thank Judith Shapiro, and profusely, for her e-mail to this effect a few days later.) At the event, sitting between Jim Peacock and Natalie Davis, hearing Cliff's responses to all the papers, and sensing the intensity of some 400 listeners engaged in the arts of participant-reception, I experienced sudden hope that anthropology and her sister disciplines might have many years of effervescence ahead.

≈

1. On Boas's knowingly impossible standards of ever more exacting comparative evidence and translation, see Arnold Krupat's "Irony in Anthropology: The Work of Franz Boas," in *Modernist Anthropology: From Fieldwork to Text,* ed. Marc Manganaro (Princeton: Princeton University Press, 1990), 133–45. For fresh senses of irony in anthropology overall (or as I'd say, "underall"), see James Fernandez and Mary Huber, eds., *Irony in Action: Anthropology, Practice, and the Moral Imagination* (Chicago: University of Chicago Press, 2001).

2. George Steiner, *On Difficulty* (New York: Oxford University Press, 1978), following up on his *After Babel.* On opera and anthropological hybridities (including pastiche), see James Boon, *Verging on Extra-vagance: Anthropology, History, Religion, Literature, Arts . . . Showbiz* (Princeton: Princeton University Press, 1999), 8–13, 284–86.

3. Clifford Geertz, *Bali: Interprétation d'une culture* (Paris: Editions Gallimard), chap. 5. The fond remark on Javanese is in LK, 10. On catalogue rhetoric and comparative interpretation, American-style, see Boon, *Verging,* xiii, 267–76, passim.

4. James Boon, *Other Tribes, Other Scribes* (New York: Cambridge University Press, 1982), 21.

5. Geertz's "Culture and Social Change: The Indonesian Case" (*Man N.S.* 19 [1884]: 511–32), does nearly demonize (and justifiably) "economism"—reductionist assumptions riddling both development planners and Marxist theorists in their not-dissimilar reactions to his *Agricultural Involution;* an earlier theoretical foe, similarly reductionist, was "psychologism." For more thoughts on "relative relativism," see Boon, *Verging,* xv, chap. 1; Boon, *Other Tribes,* chap. 3.

6. I cite *Lady Chatterley's Lover*'s lapse (vaulting?) into brogue from memory—more authoritative (if we believe Harold Bloom on his) than the text. That I am not native to this dialect may cause pause. On rereading (both style and substance) Geertz and others, see James Boon, "Showbiz as a Cross-Cultural System: Circus and Song, Garland and Geertz, Rushdie, Mordden . . . and More," *Cultural Anthropology* 15, no. 3 (2000): 424–56; and Boon, *Verging,* chaps. 1, 3–6. Space restrictions here preclude noting other recent studies of Geertz's work.

7. Weber's extravagant parsing and etymologizing of *Beruf* expands over many foot-

notes in his *The Protestant Ethic and the Spirit of Capitalism;* several complete translations into English now exist, including Stephen Kalberg's (Los Angeles: Roxbury Publishing, 2002; see 180–87). Space restrictions here preclude adequate notes (if such a thing is imaginable) on Weber, or even on his notes. Following Geertz, I have stressed the challenge of Weberian sweep in four books: *Verging; Affinities and Extremes* (Chicago: University of Chicago Press, 1990); *Other Tribes;* and *The Anthropological Romance of Bali* (New York: Cambridge University Press, 1977); all of these try to address comparative institutional specifics. Navigating Weber's vastness can be daunting; on Weber's contrastive *Verstehens* of a "calling to commensality," see James Boon, "The Cross-Cultural Kiss: Edwardian and Earlier, Postmodern and Beyond," *Skomp Distinguished Lectures in Anthropology,* University of Indiana, 1997.

8. See also AL, 255–56; and re-peruse Geertzwerk on back to *Negara* (1980), *Islam Observed* (1967), and the essays on "new states" in *Interpretation of Cultures,* an earlier appraisal of what has become today's "world in pieces" (AL, chap. 11).

REFERENCES

Boon, James A. 1999. *Verging on Extra-vagance : Anthropology, History, Religion, Literature, Arts . . . Showbiz.* Princeton: Princeton University Press.
Geertz, Clifford. [1960] 1976. *The Religion of Java.* Chicago: University of Chicago Press.
———. 1983. *Local Knowledge: Further Essays in Interpretive Anthropology.* New York: Basic Books.
———. 2000. Available Light: Anthropological Reflections on Philosophical Topics. Princeton: Princeton University Press.

Clifford Geertz on Time and Change

W
ONDERING HOW TO TELL of his life and thoughts as an anthropologist, Clifford Geertz wrote:

> Time, this sort of time, part personal, part vocational, part political, part
> (whatever that might mean) philosophical, does not flow like some vast river
> catching up all its tributaries and heading toward some final sea or cataract,
> but as larger and smaller streams, twisting and turning and now and then
> crossing, running together for a while, separating again. Nor does it move
> in shorter and longer cycles and durations, superimposed one upon another
> as a complex wave for an harmonic analyst to factor out. It is not history
> one is faced with, nor biography, but a confusion of histories, a swarm
> of biographies. There is order in it all of some sort, but it is the order of a
> squall or a street market.[1]

That quotation suggests some of the reasons Clifford Geertz has had such
a powerful impact on historians, immensely creative for some, irritating
and frightening for others. In past years, he has taught historians especially how to make sense of repeated forms of telling behavior—the restless movement and confrontations of a Moroccan marabout, the blood
and betting of the Balinese cockfight. In future years, his work can provide historians with ways of thinking about and metaphors for describing
longer-term change in a world that is both precariously post-colonial and
threatened with universal monarchy.

Clifford Geertz's techniques for observing, understanding, and writing
about Indonesia and Morocco burst upon the horizon of historians like
fireworks back in the 1970s. Two concerns drew younger historians to
his work. One was the need to understand ceremonial, liturgical, festive
and other forms of symbolic behavior. Social historians often ignored
these behaviors as "irrational," or reduced them to practical uses (like
group solidarity); confessional historians simply took them for granted as
true and God-given. For me and my students, it was Cliff's *Interpretation
of Cultures* of 1973 that brought the message of the multiple meanings

of religious belief and practice. How many clues these essays gave us as we struggled to understand, say, the strange almost liturgical forms of religious violence in the sixteenth century.

The second appeal of Cliff's work to historians lay in its focus on a limited space—a town, a compound, a bazaar—and an intensely significant and observable local event, out of which could be teased a world of meaning and an enduring style of living. I am sure Cliff has had enough of historians who place themselves under the banner of his Balinese cockfight and thick description—sometimes delivering only sparse and ephemeral stories—but it is nonetheless true that his essays are, like Carlo Ginzburg's *The Cheese and the Worms,* among the founding texts for North American microhistory.

Such moves had their critics among historians. What about historical change? they asked. Anthropology may be just fine for depicting systems and their fissures, but how does it account for, say, the change from the domination of the peoples of the East Indies by the Dutch to the domination of the archipelago by the Jakarta-based Indonesian government? Cliff himself recalls this objection in a 1990 essay: "There seem to be historians, their anthropological educations having ended with Malinowski or begun with Lévi-Strauss, who think that anthropologists, mindless of change or hostile to it, present static pictures of immobile societies scattered about in remote corners of the inhabited world."[2]

Change is everywhere in the writings of Clifford Geertz. It is part of his story of peoples, communities, economic sites, religions, scholarly disciplines, and individual lives. The change is usually initiated or described as coming from outside rather than emerging from an instability or conflict within the town, polity, religious formation, or person. The "forces" or big processes of change are the familiar ones: in *Islam Observed* of 1968, they are "the industrial revolution, Western intrusion and domination, the decline of the aristocratic principle of government, and the triumph of radical nationalism." These are Cliff's shorthand ways of helping readers understand what intervened between "the classical styles" of Islamic sensibility and practice in Morocco and Indonesia and "the scripturalist interlude." In 1995, in reflecting on the political style of Indonesia and Morocco as these independent countries maneuver for a place in the world, he draws upon "the rearrangements of global power relations, trade flows and cultural affiliations that the decolonization of Asia and Africa set in motion between the late forties and the early eighties." Decolonization, along with global migration, is also a critical variable in shifts in the discipline of anthropology and the goals and worries of its practitioners in the late twentieth century: "the transformation," as he says in *Works and Lives,* "partly juridical, partly ideological, partly real, of the people anthropologists mostly write about, from colonial subjects to sovereign citizens."[3]

Cliff's originality in describing change lies not in identifying well-known variables or in establishing long chains of causation—a procedure he rejects even on expository grounds—but in other intellectual and literary actions. He makes an up-close analysis of the agents and impact of external change on whatever cultural complex, production, or set of lives he is describing, noting with elegant precision the signs of "before" and "after," and yet finding that a fundamental fashion of local doing and thinking is surprisingly durable. Further, he reveals the possibilities in and viabilities of these durable styles and practices so as to undermine rigid stage theories and other linear models of historical change. Instead he offers fresh metaphors for imagining historical movement.

To illustrate some of these points, who can forget Cliff's contrast between the Moroccan Sefrou he knew in 1963 and the Sefrou he saw in 1986? The walled market town, with its age-old population of Arabs and Jews, whose variations and dissimulations could still be put together in a book with ethnographic chapter headings, had given way to a swollen population of old Arab families—"the real Sefrouis"—and Berber newcomers from the countryside, the specialized sections of town dissolved into diffuse urban sprawl. What kind of order could he make of that "instant jumble?" he asked himself, feeling that the transformed Sefrou had also changed him as knower.[4]

And yet Cliff does find centuries-old continuities after all, in the ways power is lodged in personages: in marabouts with their baraka, scholars with their competing claims to legitimation, judges and other notables of the mosques, the markets, and the government offices, all struggling for and constantly shifting alliances. The loyalty and friendship underlying "bargained-out dependency relations," is still at the heart of things as it was five hundred years before in the days of the Moroccan traveler "Leo Africanus."[5] There are other enduring styles, moderated, adjusted, recast in new circumstances, but still recognizable. On the political level, it is the same old task: "building up something that looks like governance out of locally anchored personal loyalties." Muhammad V transformed the sultanate in the first years of Moroccan independence but succeeded because he assumed the persona of the maraboutic king. In torn Sefrou, the conflict between old and new inhabitants was fought out, if not resolved, in 1986, on common turf: the color of buildings, the facades of private dwellings, of great moments in a land where architecture has long been a feature of morality.[6]

Cliff's treatment of Indonesia has a similar mixture of transformative ruptures and long-term social, aesthetic, and religious styles, which shift, react, and persist. In *Works and Lives* and *After the Fact,* he describes the play between historical change, large and local, on the one hand, and the anthropological approach and literary style of individual anthropologists on the other. Precise historical context is of critical importance in setting the objectives for the anthropologist. For Ruth Benedict, the occasion for *Patterns of Culture* was the interwar quest by anthropologists for basic patterns in human societies; for *The Chrysanthemum and the Sword,* the political concerns with Japan during and after World War II. But Cliff's brilliant chapter depicts Benedict embarked throughout these different contexts, from start to finish, on moral satire of Swiftian dimensions, her "rhetorical strategy" being, in Cliff's words, "the juxtaposition of the all-too-familiar [us] and the wildly exotic [them] in such a way that they change places."[7]

Cliff's self-portrait in *After the Fact* and in his Haskins lecture has the same dialectic between historical settings, style, and self. The social science atmosphere of Harvard right after the war, the interdisciplinary milieu of the University of Chicago in the 1960s, the confrontational life at the Institute for Advanced Study all shaped his plans, even while he describes himself as lighting on Indonesia and Morocco simply by good luck. Along with this story of changing institutional scenes and a some-what Chaplinesque fashion of approaching the mysteries of Javanese and Moroccan towns is the story of the early emergence and persistence of his belief that "the study of meaning, the vehicles of meaning, and the understanding of meaning" were at the heart of his anthropological re-search. In retrospect he sees himself grappling with this goal already as he worked on his doctoral dissertation, *The Religion of Java.* "The rest is postscript," he quips and recounts how he has followed the hermeneutic path for forty years, delighted to find that people in other fields were starting off in the same direction.[8]

As an admiring reader of Cliff's books, I was surprised to come upon this story of sameness in his autobiographical writings. It had seemed to me that *Peddlers and Princes, The Religion of Java,* and *Agricultural Involution* had multiple and sometimes-conflicting goals—social, func-tional, and cultural (in the sense of style, affect, and ideas)—and that the study of meaning was a new step that grew out of an early creative con-flict. Here I may be projecting from my own experience when as a social historian in 1969 I extended my study of "consciousness" to include a vast space of actions and forms and felt I had really changed.

Cliff ponders often the question of how to narrate the past: Historicizing yourself [he writes], dividing your past into periods, is an uncomfortable sort of thing to do. It is uncomfortable not just for the obvious reason that the further you move from the beginning the closer you come to the end, but because there are so many ways to do it; any particular one seems arbitrary, rooted in very little else but narrative.[9]

Already in *Islam Observed,* in 1968, he was running through the choices for explaining and narrating change—indexical (that is, following through a predetermined mark of change like the decline of magic), typological ("primitive," "medieval," "modern") and evolutionary—and finding them all wanting.[10] Certainly, Cliff's demonstration of the continuing viability, flexibility, and creativity of core cultural styles would place him in opposition to any linear evolutionary scheme. Likewise with his treatment of bazaars in Java and Morocco as tenable economic and information-swapping institutions; he is willing to use the concept of "modern" in *After the Fact,* but only in the plural as "modernities."

Especially interesting are Cliff's experiments with new ways of conceiving and telling about time and change. Already in a study of 1968 he found a fresh language for describing an economic situation that most historians would hastily characterize as "static," or "stagnant." In the seventeenth to the nineteenth centuries, the Dutch "superimposed their colonial economy" on the productive and labor-intensive wet-rice agricultural system of the island of Java. During the nineteenth century, sugar production took land away from the peasants of the rice paddies and brought profits to the Dutch. At the same time, the Javanese population soared and rice production increased.[11]

Cliff accounts for this by a process of "involution," a term drawn from discussions of artistic design and which his keen eye for patterns in behavior led him to apply to agricultural and social practices. In involution, a fully formed cultural pattern, rather than remaining static or breaking and turning into something new, "continues to develop by becoming internally more complicated." With no increase in land and no alternative, say, in manufacture, the Javanese peasants elaborated on their land-intensive patterns so as to incorporate their expanded numbers. The paddy fields became places of "internal elaboration and ornateness; technical hairsplitting, and unending virtuosity":

And this "late Gothic" quality of agriculture increasingly pervaded the whole rural economy: tenure systems grew more intricate, tenancy relationships more complicated; cooperative labor arrangements more complex—all in an effort to provide everyone with some niche, however small, in the over-all system.[12]

We see Cliff's temporal imagination at work twenty years later as he characterizes Lévi-Strauss's body of writings. Cliff rejects current views that they should be understood in terms of linear progress—first Lévi-Strauss studied nature, then culture, then behavior, then thought—or that, on the contrary, they should be seen as an unchanging structuralist program turned on different subjects one after another. Instead the movement is "centrifugal," and *Tristes Tropiques*—a midstream book, which fits neither scheme—is the "arch-text." As Cliff puts it: all Lévi-Strauss's works, even those published before *Tristes Tropiques,* can be viewed "as partial unpackings of it, developments of particular strains present, embryonically at least and usually much more fully than that, in this, the most multiplex of his writings."[13]

When I read this, I begin to think about whether a historian could use an arch-text or an arch-event not to erase the chronology of a sequence, but to imagine a very different way that something in the middle could be related to what went before and what came afterward.

Finally, Cliff's book *After the Fact* is a fascinating effort to reconfigure time. Its order is not that of a mere squall, to return to the quotation with which I opened these remarks, nor is it as hard to fathom as the crisscrossings at a bazaar. But it does have multiple histories and biographies, as sites, persons, decades, and themes are returned to with different questions and perspectives and as Clifford Geertz appears in all of them, "coming and going and knocking about," "trying to find [his] feet in all sorts of places," "go[ing] if not forward at least onward."[14] To his words of self-description, we would add: observing and interpreting things deeply and anew, opening ways of understanding people close to home and far away, telling us about the world in a prose whose rhythm captures voice and mind, and writing about himself with the humor and detachment that are the true mark of greatness.

NOTES

1. Clifford Geertz, *After the Fact: Two Countries, Four Decades, One Anthropologist* (Cambridge: Harvard University Press, 1995), 2.

2. Clifford Geertz, "History and Anthropology," initially published in *New Literary History* in 1990, and reprinted in *Available Light* (Princeton: Princeton University Press, 2000), 118–19.

3. Clifford Geertz, *Islam Observed: Religious Development in Morocco and Indonesia*

(New Haven: Yale University Press, 1968), 56–57; *After the Fact,* 89; *Works and Lives: The Anthropologist as Author* (Stanford: Stanford University Press, 1988), 132.

4. Geertz, *After the Fact,* 11–17.

5. I am currently completing a book on "Leo Africanus," that is, the early-sixteenth-century traveler and diplomat as-Hasan ibn Muhammad as-Wazzan, and am finding Clifford Geertz's writings very helpful in putting questions to my texts of 500 years ago.

6. Geertz, *After the Fact,* 27, 29, 33, 58–59, 152–64; *Islam Observed,* 74–82.

7. Geertz, *Works and Lives,* 106.

8. Geertz, *After the Fact,* 104, 114, 119; Clifford Geertz, "A Life of Learning," The Charles Homer Haskins Lecture for 1999, ACLS Occasional Paper, no. 45, 1999, 14.

9. Geertz, *After the Fact,* 109.

10. Geertz, *Islam Observed,* 57–59; also, *After the Fact,* 1–2.

11. Clifford Geertz, *Agricultural Involution: The Process of Ecological Change in Indonesia* (Berkeley: University of California Press, 1968), chap. 4.

12. Geertz, *Agricultural Involution,* 80–82. Geertz's use of "late Gothic" evokes Johann Huyzinga's celebrated book, *The Waning of the Middle Ages: A Study of the Forms of Life, Thought, and Art in France and the Netherlands in the XIVth and XVth Centuries,* which had first appeared in Dutch just after World War I and in English translation in 1924, with many subsequent editions.

13. Geertz, *Works and Lives,* 32.

14. Ibid., 134–35.

Happenstance and Patterns

CLIFFORD GEERTZ EXEMPLIFIES the interpretive mind at its best, the anthropologist finding himself here or there, in a situation that seems half familiar, half utterly strange, himself often uncertain which is which. Sometimes finding himself in the middle of those situations, sometimes at the edge, often not sure which is which, Geertz, cast as Homo Anthropologicus is having, and spending the time of his life interpreting What's What. In all these ways, Homo Interpretes is also an actor, an agent provocateur, a deft negotiator engaged in finding/giving an account, a reckoning of The Scene that might, as he puts it, make sense of sensibility. "Interpreter": the etymology derives from Latin, *inter pres,* a go-between, a negotiator, a broker. The anthropologist living in the field, crafting the right phrase or negotiating with his academic clan, is engaged in a practical activity. Thought is, as Geertz says, a moral act; moral acts are social; they have political presuppositions and implications.

Once upon a time, the activity of interpretation was treated as observational and speculative. The anthropologist was passive in the field, active in his study, in both cases Mind at work discovering underlying forms of Societies (Cultures). After his initiation in the field, the anthropologist was set to become a solitary scholar, construing his notes in order to decipher his society's structures, his culture's coded system of signs and symbols. Unlike the original etymological understanding of interpretation as fundamentally active and transactional, the metaphors of unveiling, deciphering, construing posed a metaphysical dilemma: either there is a basic Fact of The Matter that the anthropologist attempts to discover and articulate . . . or his descriptive analyses are shadows cast (on what?) by a beholder (in which of the beholder's *personae*?). Geertz has shown us how to avoid the hopeless heroics of facing such unresolvable metaphysical dilemmas: take a detour around the dead-end metaphors of the solitary observing, deciphering mind . . . or, better: so multiply metaphors that the sting of any one set causes no inflammation.

Geertz's essays have shown us how to bypass the mind-deadening theory-defining "isms" that formed the combat zones where academic careers were won or lost. Many of these theories quickly escalated to metatheories that were implausibly ranged as forced options: reductivism vs. constructivism, biologism vs. psychologism, phenomenology vs. science, behaviorism vs. culturalism, structuralism vs. functionalism, universalism vs. pluralistic localism, relativism and anti-relativism and anti anti-relativism, and so forth, all ranged to fight in endless unresolvable battles on an otherwise empty plain, without anyone being clear about what, if anything, might be at stake. Like Dewey, Geertz has taken us through these oppositions, analyzed their sources, placed them in a larger conceptual field, reconciled/overcome their apparent opposition, and then acknowledged them again. His own strategy against schemes and systems of dichotomies has a characteristic plot. He first shows that the oppositions are mutually dependent. For instance, the claims of radical relativism presuppose enough common understanding to locate differences: identifying structural units presupposes hypotheses about their functions, and functional hypotheses occur in a structured field; the task of defining individuated units of behavior presupposes a system of cultural categories. Having defused oppositions, Geertz then introduces third and fourth mediating categories, and then—with a deft turn—preserves the insights of the original opposition. There is, as Geertz has himself remarked, Dewey in his method. But unlike Dewey, and like Hegel, Geertz has a historical understanding of the rise and fall of the opposition of "isms"; and unlike Hegel, and like Dewey, Geertz's historical understanding casts no metaphysical shadows. Unfortunately both Hegel and Dewey were burdened with a dense and muddy style whose vague abstractions were surprisingly unreflective. Apparently lacking irony, their philosophical confidence remained unperturbed by self-criticism. Unlike the philosophers, Geertz undermines premature neatness with a wealth of examples and inimitable ironic asides, construing ancient epics and sacred texts, interpreting artworks and locating the insights of the latest intellectual *wunderkinden* ("Deep Hanging Out," "The State of the Art").

Having undermined and reconstituted what is living and what is dead in the standard fashionable "isms," Geertz has also put the apparently interminable wars between the faculties to rest. He has sorted out and adjudicated the claims, appropriations, and renunciations of anthropology by historians, legal and political theorists, philosophers, and natural scientists, rejecting "the historicist/scientist dichotomy" . . . ['deja vu all over again']" and put them all in their commingled and opposing places, welcoming help wherever he can get it but firmly refusing reductive domination whenever it appears. Starting from a modest recognition of Where One Is and a circumscribed sense of what one is trying to understand— "less than Everything, less than "Society," "Man, "Woman," or some other grand elusive upper-case entity"—Geertz reveals his distrust for the grandiose and his taste for the specific. As usual, the best way to convey Geertz's message is to quote him: "The conjoining of History and Anthropology is not a matter of fusing two academic fields into Something-or-Other, but redefining them in terms of another. . . . Sorting things out into . . . what happened and what we can say about what happened will not, in the end, really do. . . . In the end nothing will really do. . . . [To understand] history-anthropology relations in action is not a deliberate tacking between variant modes of discourse, but an unintended, almost *happenstance* convergence of them upon a common concern: the enmeshment of meaning in power."[1]

I want to add an item to our wish list for Geertz's next act. The motif of the respective roles of chance and happenstance in the unfolding of a culture's history—or for that matter, of an individual life—is played out in every phase of Geertz's thought. Yet—perhaps profoundly influenced by the happenstance of his early work in Bali—he is also a persistent and even relentless pattern-finder. Despite his impatience with forced oppositions, the implicit tension between the pervasiveness of chance and the continuing discovery of patterns has been a driving theme in his work. The theme is explicit in his discussion of odds-on gambling in "Deep Play, Notes on the Balinese Cockfight"; it reaches a crescendo in "Passage and Accident" and in his more recent philosophically reflective writings. The dramas of happenstance have always been present in his vivid ethnographic descriptions: the unexpected, unrehearsed events following a police raid on a Balinese cockfight, the authorial pride of a Javanese informant,[2] the multiply intersecting dramas and rituals of nineteenth century Balinese governance show a people struggling to encompass— to integrate—the inevitability of chance coincidence in a culture in which every event, every turn of object evinces a plenitude of significance and meaning. As he tells it, for such cultures, no leaf falls without a message . . . everything, but absolutely everything has a place in a significant pattern. The interplay between the cockfight and the patterned rituals of gambling, the independent but interlocked multiple "political" organizations serve as star examples of the integration of happenstance and pattern. On the one hand, as luck would have it, many independent lines happen to coincide in the outcome of the cockfight. That's why it can be a betting matter. On the other, there is a pattern—an implicit rule—in the permissible alignment of odds in the betting, and that pattern, right in the middle of a chance event, replicates and reinforces the pervasive social and meaningful configuration of the culture. The theme develops the searing contrast—and the Balinese resolution—between the jolting recognition of the pervasiveness of chance and happenstance (on the one hand) and the universal verve, indeed the obsession with finding patterns, significantly meaning-laden patterns.

If chance incidents only involved a set of contingencies along one narrative line, they could be significantly integrated by stretching probability. But the fortuitous, accidental conjunction of a set of independent narrative lines, each of them itself contingent is another matter altogether.[3] The kind of happenstance that co-incidentally, accidentally conjoins several independent contingent narrative lines evokes some of our profound existential anxieties. We fear the pervasiveness of chance in matters of great personal or political moment, just when the hope—the need—of guiding intelligence is greatest. For contemporary liberals, there is the further moral chill: the effects of chance aren't always egalitarian. Even if there is plenty of chance to go around, its impact is more far-reaching on some people, some cultures, some economic classes than on others. Just when we think luck has been on our side, we see how inconstant it is. It is not only a matter of being subject to the erratic turn of events. Pervasive chance undermines the very idea of agency, let alone (what is confidently called) "rational agency." When we recognize the extent—the scope— of the unintended consequences of our actions, the claims of intentional and meaningful purposive action begins to seem naively childish, if not downright churlish. To be sure, chance happenstance is by no means all there is; after all, even chaos is only recognizable against the background of the expectation of a particular order or of a consequential narrative. Even advanced postmodern films are charged by recognizable regularities.

Geertz has been the master dramatist of the ramifications of cliff-hanging chance events. But he is also a master diviner of cultural patterns and of the patterns of internally and externally impelled dynamics of cultural transformations. (Let's have done with the critical complaints that Geertz's ethnographies present cultures as overly unified, simplified and static themes, modes or styles. Far from being reductive, he has consistently analyzed the dynamics of intracultural conflicts between priests and peddlers, urban people and villagers, high and low art.) A culture's continuously transformative and transforming expressions of such conflicts *are* the ingredients of its forms and structures. The dynamic relations among events pervades the dynamics of interpretation. Tracing the drama of such transformations, a Geertz ethnography follows the shifts in the continuously negotiated and contested character—and even the boundaries—of a culture. As the case requires, the organizing scheme of an interpretation may be economic, political, metaphysical, or psychological; it may take the form of history or a drama, a statistical table or a sacred text . . . most likely, all of the above. The emphasis may rest on kinship structures (*Kinship in Bali*), on statistical correlations (*Agricultural Involution*), the multilayered turns of multiperspectival dramatic narratives (*Negara*), the complex patterns manifest in the interaction— the fusion—of religion, law, ideology, and politics (*Islam Observed, The Interpretation of Culture*, and *Meaning and Order in Moroccan Society*).

Geertz has, in all of these ethnographical studies, vividly analyzed the integrative strategic resolutions between the disquieting interpenetration of pervasive chance and pervasive patterns: the deep play of Balinese cockfight gambling, the dramas of the shifts in their multiple political allegiances and the geo-political dynamics of legal, political, and economic organization in Sefrou, Morocco. Those resolutions may be very well for the Balinese and Moroccans. But the metaphysical problems that surround the opposition of sheer happenstance and constitutive patterns are not merely problems about the limits of our understanding of causation, and they cannot always be resolved by symbolic rituals. They are direct, practical questions for interpretive anthropologists. What is the stance of the interpretive anthropologist, acutely aware of the chance happenstance coincidences of his fieldwork—indeed of his own intellectual history—but who is nevertheless committed to elucidating "the patterns of culture?"

The motif of the pervasiveness of happenstance has moved to the forefront as a central motif in Geertz's recent philosophical and Zeitgeistliche autobiographical reflections on the methods of multidisciplinary cultural studies (*Local Knowledge* and *Available Light*). He recognizes that the events of his life, the turns of his thought could have gone this way or that. . . . It so happened that his teacher at Antioch was George Geiger . . . it so happened that Geiger was Dewey's last graduate student. . . . Speaking of his first fieldwork, he remarks, "Once again I caught the wave. . . . As improbably and casually as we had become anthropologists, and just about as innocently, we became Indonesianists." We happened to be present when the police raided an illegal cockfight, . . . and we happened to run into a villager's compound, and we all managed to support one another's stories . . . and after that, everything changed. . . . As luck would have it, my informant was—or wanted to be—a writer and so I lent him my typewriter . . . but . . . one day it happened . . . and so on.

Must Geertz follow Isaiah Berlin and Charles Taylor in classifying the world of happenstance and that of patterns as among the irreconcilable, incommensurable forms of life?[4] In this case, there is no escaping the need for a resolution. Consider the possibility of a world—a form of life—whose essential thematic interpretive heuristic is: "The meaning of every event is unintelligible. Events involve coincidental intersections of sequences of events that are themselves disjointed, unpatterned, unintended and unpredictable." Such a world would not have any stable practices; it is not even coherent. A culture pervaded by a chance-ridden outlook would issue in a life entirely composed of Ionesco conversations randomly interspersed with Beckett reflections. Even if such a form of life were conceivable, we are not—in this case—able to choose between chaos and order, as if they were two comprehensive, but incompatible ways of life. Neither individuals nor cultures can choose between a life permeated by chance conjunctions of time and place and one patterned by regularities of strongly defined social roles, friendships, and feuds, a mode of life that exhibits and largely follows a pattern that significantly organizes the movements of individuals and the meanings of institutions.

Nor can the contrast between happenstance and pattern be assimilated to other, more safely theoretical, less existentially vertiginous contrasts: between subjectivity and objectivity for instance, or between free will and necessity, or phenomenology and science. As we experience them, happenstance and pattern are mutually pervasive. They inhabit the same terrain. The reductively simplistic psychological suggestion that the quest for patterns is a function of the terror of chance only introduces another pattern, as does the apparently soothing recommendation that looking for patterns in chance events elicits them.

Geertz himself exhibits and reflects on another kind of resolution of chance and patterns. His style is, as Richard Shweder has said, spectacular. It can't be ignored. The style is the man; the medium is the message. The sentences of Geertz's later autobiographical and zeitgeist-mapping essays are palimpsests of distinctive moments of a complex thought. They twist and turn, leap and bound; they are interrupted by tangential asides. They are lyrical yet earthy, directly confrontational yet evasive. They are self-conscious exhibitions and commentaries on the very process of thought, exemplifying assertion, qualification, reflection and counter-reflection on sheer happenstance, even as it affects the authorial stance. Here I stand; like many others, I might well have thought otherwise, and may yet do so, but for the moment . . . here is how it seems to me. Asking whether the good fortune of his "charmed life, in a charmed time" is still available for young anthropologists, Geertz says, "It is difficult to be certain. The matter is *sub judice*. . . . There does seem to be a fair amount of malaise about. . . . [I]t is probably not altogether wise just now to take unnecessary chances. . . . I do not know how much of this is accurate, how much it presents a passing condition . . . how much an alteration, rich and strange, in the structure of chance and possibilities." He reflects that he no longer advises younger colleagues to stay loose, take risks, follow their own bent. This is not merely a modest fallibilism; it is, in the reflection and the rhythm of the prose, the practical, transactional and morally sensitive recognition of the fusion of chance and pattern. Speaking of the lessons he learned in fieldwork Geertz says, "I remain calm and unfazed [about the culture wars, about the downfalling of anthropology and just about everything else] not so much above the battle as beside it, skeptical of its very assumptions." He adds, "and the rest is post script, the working out of happenstance and fate." But in truth, the rest is the beginning of the next act, the next turn of thought. Geertz accepts the moral obligation he enjoins: to continue conversation, to reflect on the tragedy and farce of having to address the endless return of repressed oppositions. Think of Geertz—the man and his style—as exemplifying Dewey's philosophic generosity, Isaiah Berlin's erudition, and Mark Twain's wry ironic asides, "the working out of happenstance fate."

NOTES

1. Clifford Geertz, *Available Light: Anthropological Reflections on Philosophical Topics* (Princeton: Princeton University Press, 2000), 127–28.

2. Clifford Geertz, "Thinking as a Moral Act: Ethical Dimensions of Anthropological Field Work in the New States," *Antioch Review* 27 (1968).

3. See Aristotle, *Physics*, 2, 196b 30ff.; and James Lenman, "Consequentialism and Cluelessness," *Philosophy and Public Affairs* 24, no. 4 (2000).

4. See Isaiah Berlin, *The Sense of Reality* (New York: Farrar, Straus and Giroux, 1997); and Charles Taylor, "Conflicts of Modernity," chapter 25 in his *Sources of the Self* (Cambridge: Harvard University Press, 1989).

Geertz's Concept of Culture in Historical Context
How He Saved the Day and Maybe the Century

MY OBJECTIVE IS TO HIGHLIGHT one of Geertz's contributions by reminding us of historical context. I contend that he saved anthropology and the wider society from a great loss at a dangerous point in anthropology's history.[1]

In 1960 Clifford Geertz published his first book, *The Religion of Java.* The previous year he had published an important article in the *American Anthropologist,* "Ritual and Social Change: A Javanese Example." The book, which was essentially his doctoral dissertation at Harvard with theoretical discussions deleted and a new descriptive conclusion, paralleled in some ways the several works of Max Weber, such as *Religion of India* and *Religion of China,* etc., which were parts of the larger *Afsatze Zur Religionssoziologie.* The article, as we know, introduced anthropologists to a concept of culture based on the theories of Talcott Parsons and Pitirim Sorokin, that culture was a system of symbols, ideas, and values, integrated in a logico-meaningful mode, in contrast to a causal-functional mode that better characterized social systems. Geertz provided a suggestive analysis of a Javanese funeral whose tensions, he argued, derived from a clash between the two kinds of systems.

What else was happening in anthropology at this time—the late 1950s, early 1960s? Two things: deaths and births. In 1960 Clyde Kluckhohn died. In 1958 Alfred Kroeber gave a swan song at the American Anthropological Association meetings, then died in the early 1960s. Kluckhohn and Kroeber (1952) had authored the scholarly survey of concepts of culture and represented a humanistic and holistic heritage of American cultural anthropology, which drew on German philosophical traditions transmitted by Boas and others. With their deaths, anthropology lost champions of a humanistic and holistic perspective on culture.

Around the same time, new schools were born. Two that had great impact were structuralism and ethnoscience. Structuralism was announced by Claude Lévi-Strauss in his 1955 essay "The Structural Study of Myth," and ethnoscience, otherwise known as componential analysis or cognitive anthropology, broached by Ward Goodenough in his 1956 article "Residence Rules" in the *Southwestern Journal of Anthropology,* followed by work by Conklin, Frake, Lounsbury, and others (see Goodenough's "Componential Analysis" in *Science,* 1967, volume 156). While differing greatly, the two schools shared similarities. Both focused on thought, the mind, either of an individual or a collectivity, as embodied in symbols—language, mythology, kinship systems, and terminologies. Both laid bare the logical structure of these systems. And both tended to see those logics as disembodied, as abstracted from life and action, so that the structures could be analyzed mathematically and technically, by formulas and even computers.

Why was this a dangerous situation for anthropology? A vacuum was opening up with the death of champions and a decline of a great tradition of culture. Contending to fill this vacuum were these new schools such as structuralism and ethnoscience, which were having a large impact. Lévi-Strauss's impact is widely known, but within anthropology ethnoscience, too, attracted much attention, for example, dominating the special publication list of AAA during the early 1960s. Boasting strengths, their weaknesses were notable. Ethnoscience especially narrowed the concept of culture to ethnosemantics and narrowed ethnographic fieldwork to procedures of eliciting terms from informants so as to define their cognitive models. Structuralism is vast in compass but also reduces culture to cognition, of a sort. Neither ethnoscience nor structuralism treated the dynamics of whole societies, nations, for example, or global movements and the meaningful or cultural dimensions of them. Nor did they sustain the rich humanistic insights of Benedict (1943), Mead (1953), or Kroeber (1944) who, whatever their excesses, confronted large patterns, be they Native American, Japanese, Soviet, or great waves of history, and did so with dash, flair, and comparative breadth. Should these be replaced by either narrow techniques or by brilliant but abstruse models? Anthropology was in danger of selling its birthright for thin porridge.

Geertz to the rescue. As the grand old traditions died and the barbarians or flâneurs threatened at the gate, he brought forward a perspective that at once sustained and developed the great tradition while providing a workable alternative to the challengers. He did this by adapting from a sociological tradition not previously salient in American cultural anthropology. This was the Weberian tradition, filtered through Talcott Parsons, now shaped and anthropologized by Geertz. This is not to reduce

Geertz to Weber or Parsons but to acknowledge their influence, as he does himself and as can be traced through his graduate student papers in the 1950s prepared in seminars with Parsons, on down to his published works. My emphasis here, though, is not origins of Geertz's thinking, which is complex, and on which he himself has elaborated somewhat, in *After the Fact* (1995), and in his Haskins lecture at the American Council of Learned Societies (1999), but rather on what he contributed at this point in history.[2]

What did he contribute? Most importantly, a concept of culture and a demonstration of the importance of culture in life as a whole and especially as a way of defining meaning and shaping meaning in the midst of action and change.

In asserting this, I will confine my observations to his published sources during the period in question, that is, the decade extending from 1959 with his article on the Javanese funeral to his essay on the Balinese cockfight published in 1972. These and other essays are collected in *The Interpretation of Cultures,* published in 1973. I also have in mind the books during this period, including his first, *Religion of Java,* and previous and subsequent ones (1956, 1963, 1965, 1968, 1980, 1983, 2000). I was never a student of Geertz, so my knowledge is based primarily on published and unpublished works (plus, I might note, a delicious conversation in the field with one of his informants).

What underlying frame of reference may one abstract from Geertz's varied works? "Action," is basic. From human action, be it a funeral, a cockfight, or a revolution or meditation, a community or a movement, one abstracts meanings: winks; a wink is a meaningful twitch. Detecting meaning entails "interpretation," or "thick description," and such interpretations are framed by a concept of culture, which one might quickly define as logico-meaningfully interrelated ideas, symbols, and values that bestow meaning. That concept of culture evolved through Geertz's writings. In his 1959 paper on the funeral, culture is a system of symbols, while by his 1972 paper on the cockfight, culture is a text one reads over an informants' shoulder. At other points in that decade, culture is a molding and shaping configuration, as in "Religion as a Cultural System." But always there's meaning, and meaning is bestowed by interrelated symbols, values, and ideas.

Such configurations of meaning boast a certain autonomy from social structures and processes, a point British social anthropologists such as Mary Douglas[3] never accepted from Geertz, but the meaning configurations never become hermetically sealed, abstracted logical structures a la structuralism/ethnoscience. Rather they engage life, challenge and conflict with processes in society, whether local as in the funeral, or national and economic as in business and revolution.

What did this Geertzian notion of culture add or subtract? To the American cultural anthropology heritage, Geertz added a more limited and precise yet still pregnant concept of culture. Rather than a comprehensive rather vague label for all that is human and not biological, the notion holding sway from Tylor to Kroeber, Geertz's notion follows the Parsonsian view of culture as essentially ideational. To the British social anthropology heritage, he added this elaborated ideational dimension, distinct from yet dynamically interacting with social forces. To Weberian origins, he added anthropology—ethnography, life, the world, and especially the contemporary world. Culture through Geertz's influence became essential in understanding the new nations, Islam, politics, economic development, and history. Could this plethora of uses of culture have happened with either the older sprawling notion or the newer restrictive ideas? It did not.

So, jumping to today, many of us, working in varied spheres, inside and outside anthropology, find ourselves bumping into Geertz, sometimes eerily transformed. In my work, directing a center for international studies, he is there, expressed by politicians, security analysts, K-12 teachers among the 300 schools with whom we work, legislators, business people, and culture and political brokers, such as Gordon Smith, the creator of a global interactive museum, Exploris, which is at the center of an effort to internationalize an entire region focused around a state capital, Raleigh, North Carolina. All of these draw on a concept of culture, and one reason they do is Clifford Geertz.

I should not exaggerate. Their concept of culture is not explicitly Geertzian. The concept of culture seems to follow the old diffusionist age-area hypothesis: the older idea has spread wider and deeper than the newer one. So for most of these workers outside academia, culture is not the streamlined Geertzian notion, certainly not the tendentious intellectualist transformations some of us have created even more recently, but the older vague notions that were brought forward by Margaret Mead and others. Exploris even has Mead enshrined along with Einstein, Jung, and many others in stained-glass windows replacing Christ and saints in a former church, and "culture" is used in the sense of way of life, cultures, which mix and mingle in the increasingly diverse life of everyone in the society revolving around the future manifested in the museum and surrounding evolving downtown community. Still, Geertz's concept sustained and developed the older notion within academic circles, which in turn have nourished and sustained the broader influence of culture in wider circles. What began in 1959 as a crisp refinement of a concept of culture has spread and evolved in interaction with myriad streams of life and thinking that have brought culture thinking, of various kinds, to the fore. In that wider process, Geertz work is foundational—a kind of Ghost that haunts.

That ghost is difficult to exorcise. A concluding anecdote. In a class I have taught for many years, I require a hundred or so undergraduates each year to read *Interpretations of Culture*—until this year, when I decided to drop that book and replace it with Thomas Berry's *The Great Work* (1999), which exhorts us to save the earth and ventures bold generalizations. A brilliant student, who happens to be blind, seats herself on the right hand with her dog, and challenges every bold assertion with relativisms drawn from Clifford Geertz. She (Danielle Iredale) wrote on her final exam:

> I am a radical relativist anthropologist. I believe that everything in the mental, emotional, and spiritual lives of all human beings, as well as many of the supposedly biological or otherwise objectively physical elements of human existence, stem wholly from culture.

Later, Danielle upheld her point in a formal debate at the DiPhi (Dialectical and Philosophical) Society, opposing Derek, another undergraduate from the course, who took a universalist stance.

What if Geertz had not stepped forward to revitalize and enrich the concept of culture at a critical point in anthropology's history? Conceivably we would have replaced a broad and deep heritage with a more limited paradigm, and as a consequence both developments within the discipline and influences of the culture concept in the wider society could have been stifled. A kingdom could have been lost for want of a horseshoe nail, or maybe a horse plus a nail and a knight. The discipline and the society are therefore in debt to Clifford Geertz.

CODA: THICKENING THE PLOT

History, as we know, is complex and constructed. While I stand by the version presented here—a triumphalist narrative of Geertz as the hero who saved the discipline from a road best not traveled—I would admit that other streams were flowing, other roads being paved. Following these side roads permits us also to note some histories not included in standard accounts.

Dichotomizing the Geertzian and holistic/humanistic view of culture versus the structuralist/ethnoscientist view oversimplifies. Other important movements in anthropology emerging in the 1950s and 1960s should be recalled as well. Within America was the ethnography of communication led by Dell Hymes and others. This approach kept alive Boasian interest in culture and language while grounding the linguistic turn within dynamic social process and community context. In Britain, a pathbreaking work was Edmund Leach's *Political Systems of Highland Burma* (1954). Leach here placed culture as a key factor in social process, tilting Kachin society toward democratic or authoritarian patterns, although this complex analysis emphasized primarily social change, with culture as only a factor and viewed primarily as content for social process rather than as a framing paradigm. Later, in *Culture and Communication* (1976), Leach would employ the term "culture" in a more developed way consonant with his neostructuralism. Coming from the Manchester school led by Max Gluckman, Victor Turner's *Schism and Continuity in an African Society* (1957) focused on ritual as a symbolic process correlated with complex and dynamic social process, an analysis also highly developed around that time by John Middleton (1960) and later T. O. Beidelman (1993). "Symbol" and "rite" rather than culture per se were the foci of these social anthropological studies, so that they developed nuanced insights into aspects of culture—symbol, rite, etc.—without naming them "culture" or elaborating a theory of culture as a whole, rather enriching a theory of ritual and symbols within a social anthropological tradition. Returning to the American context, specifically the Harvard context within which Geertz did his graduate work, it is worth noting roots of yet another stream, often termed "symbolic anthropology."

"Symbolic anthropology" is often identified with Chicago and especially colleagues of Geertz, notably David Schneider and Victor Turner, or students of Geertz and Schneider at Chicago (see, e.g., Patterson 2001). Schneider, like Geertz, had studied at Harvard and was influenced by Parsons but developed cultural analysis in a parallel, not identical, line. The best example is his work on kinship as a cultural system, in which he elaborated a system or premises that underlay the practices in American family life (1968). Students of Geertz and Schneider at Chicago went on to elaborate their perspectives, sometimes using the label "symbolic anthropology." Some historical interest may be served by noting the following, which, so far as I know, is not widely known. The term "symbolic anthropology" seemingly was first coined as a title of a series, "Symbolic Anthropology," published by the University of Chicago Press, beginning with a monograph by me, *Rites of Modernization* (1968), followed by a second volume by Martin Silverman. This series was launched at Princeton University simultaneously with creating a program in anthropology that explicitly focused on the study of symbols. The program and series were created by David Crabb and me, who then brought Martin Silverman from Chicago, and it ended with Silverman's volume and his and my departures from Princeton. Later, James Boon, who took the first course I taught in Anthropology at Princeton (it was also his first course in that subject), went on to Chicago, and joined, then developed, the Geertzian stream.

A converging but little known history or prehistory to this development is this, which like Geertz and Schneider is partially traceable to Parsons. In spring 1960, three first-year graduate students in the Social Anthropology department, Terrence Turner, Thomas Kirsch, and I, enrolled in a seminar on the Sociology of Religion taught by Parsons and Robert Bellah. Bellah set out a perspective, "Notes on the Systematic Study of Religion," which focused on symbols, while Parsons was also elaborating the cultural and especially "expressive symbols" dimension of his theory of action (later published as *Part IV: Theories of Society,* in 1961). Partly inspired by this Parsonsian/Bellah perspective as well as others we brought to the work, Turner, Kirsch, and I developed our own formulations as graduate students. In that seminar, Turner wrote a synthesis of the study of symbols while I worked through a case study, medieval mystics (Peacock 1969). Each of us then independently continued to work on this perspective in varied contexts; thus my first publication was in archaeology, *Academica Sinica.* Turner went on to do fieldwork in Brazil on ritual, Kirsch in Thailand on Buddhism, and I in Indonesia, focusing on ludruk, a proletarian theater. By this time, Geertz had published Religion of Java, which mentioned this form, and I sent him my field proposal, which he encouraged me to pursue. His work was hugely seminal for my project, but I also turned to other influences.

While indebted to Geertz, I found it necessary to trace in depth the communicative process by which streams of culture were born and sustained (in this case by theater—see Dell Hymes's introduction to my *Rites of Modernization*). The lack of such analysis has lain behind later critiques of Geertz (e.g., Wikan 1990) as reifying culture, and proposals for "practice" as a focus later emerged by students of Geertz (e.g., Ortner 1999).

Should one probe even more circumstantially into the background of Geertz's perspective, one could go back to his fieldwork in Java (see Fagg 1958). Geertz's fieldwork in Java was part of a team project overseen by

Douglas Oliver. Ghosts of this project still remained more than a decade later: in 1970, when I stayed with the family of Soedibdjo Markoes in the town named "Mojokuto," they were still riding the bicycle of Donald Fagg, a member of Oliver's team, who had committed suicide, but whose Harvard dissertation elaborated a cultural perspective on status and power that foreshadowed the work of Benedict Anderson on a cultural definition of power in Java (Fagg 1958). Histories remain to be written about the mutual ruminations of these team members that doubtless fed the perspective best known in association with Clifford Geertz.

DEVELOPMENT: SPREADING THE WORD

Unearthing histories reminds us of the swirls of work and talk that were going on as Geertz was publishing his work and shaping thinking about culture within anthropology and beyond, in humanistic and scholarly circles. Remarkable though understandable (and still to be plumbed) is the sociology of knowledge that would plot how and why his formulation came to stand for the many interrelated efforts; historians, for example, would routinely cite "The Cockfight" and nothing else, and scholars of religion treated "Religion as a Cultural System" rather as sacred canon. On the other hand boundaries were apparent; as noted previously, the older, broader notions of culture were the ones that spread so widely in the lay world, as when analysts explore business "cultures." Humanistic notions that were pre-anthropological still prevail in formulations such as that of D. Paul Schafer, which sets forth a policy of making culture (1998).[4] And disavowals of the concept of culture tend, also, to hearken back to older and broader notions, as among feminists who see it as patriarchal (Pollock 1988) or those who worry about its generally oppressive potential (Wikan 1998 on cultures of immigrants that result in killing of daughters by fathers or commentators at the hundredth anniversary of the Polish Ethological Society who traced how culture ignited ethnic cleansing in Eastern Europe). In these critiques, the specific formulations of Geertz are not paramount, just as they are missing, also, in the positive popularizations noted here, as in the instance of Exploris.

In short, Geertz's notion of culture had critical impact within a certain context and period, an impact that still unfolds. While one of many explorations of what one might term "culture," it is arguably the one with strongest impact during a period when anthropology and other disciplines could have lost a certain "cultural capital," if one may apply that term to "culture" itself. Culture is arguably the most distinctive resource that anthropology has brought forward in its century or so of development, and formulations that lacked either the richness or the precision and engaging exposition of Geertz could have prevailed, robbing the discipline of an inheritance rather than developing and disseminating it strategically among neighboring disciplines. In this way, it was the Geertzian rendition of culture that carried the day and saved the day.

NOTES

1. A version of this argument was presented in James L. Peacock, "The Third Stream: Weber, Parsons, Geertz," *Journal of the Anthropological Society of Oxford* 12, no. 2 (1981): 122–29. This paper summarized a brief talk I gave at the request of Godfrey Lienhardt to characterize the place of Geertz in anthropology. I made two points: first, the crucial contribution of Geertz's notion of culture at a certain point in history—a point elaborated here—and, second, relations between Geertz, Weber, and Parsons, elaborated more in that paper.

2. "The third stream" begins by quoting Clyde Kluckhohn who, as I recall it, told a group of graduate students in his history of theory course in spring 1960: "All you need to know is Boas and the French." I took him to mean that socio-cultural anthropology at that time boasted only two important streams: the American, beginning with Boas and continuing through Kroeber, Lowie, and their successors, and the French, beginning with Durkheim and continuing through British and French social anthropology to Lévi-Strauss. The third stream, I suggest, was brought by Geertz beginning in 1960 when Kluckhohn died, the summer following that course, and it inserted a Weberian inspiration via Parsons—adding a certain German perspective to the American and Franco-British. I did not reduce Geertz to Weber/Parsons but noted some parallels, to wit: "action," that is, meaningful behavior as the focal unit for analysis, "interpretation" (Weber's Verstehen) by placing behavior in a framework of meaning defined by the actor (e.g., translating twitches into winks, to use Geertz's analogy in "Thick Description"), a definition of culture (as Geist, as system, as text) as framework of meaning, a premise that culture is both superior and autonomous to society, and a mode of generalizing through highlighting distinctive features of instances rather than averaging statistically across instances (ideal types and ethnographic portrayal in contrast to surveys and experiments). Geertz's approach both drew on other sources, especially philosophical and literary, and transcended this "stream." But he did join it, learn from it, and enrich it at certain points, some of which can be traced through papers he wrote while at Harvard and, following fieldwork, at MIT.

3. Mary Douglas said this in reviewing *Interpretation of Cultures* (*Times Literary Supplement* 8 [August 1975]): "Clearly the boy with guts and intellectual stamina had learnt as much (or more) from mentors in sociology, philosophy, and history as from anthropologists." She comments specifically on his analysis of the Javanese funeral: "He asserts that culture is independent in the style of 'with one bound our hero was free.' The fieldwork reporting stops here." Here Douglas contrasts her Durkheimian premise that culture is grounded in society (a premise she later argued in detail in *Cultural Bias*) with the Geertzian argument that culture and society are analytically distinct and empirically independent of each other, a premise that Weber and Parsons assert, following a German philosophical tradition of according autonomous power to Geist.

4. For a review of Schafer and other recent commentaries on culture, see James L. Peacock, "Culture and the Future," *American Anthropologist* 102, no. 2 (June 2000): 361–63.

REFERENCES

Anderson, Benedict R. O'G. 1990. The Idea of Power in Javanese Culture, 17–77. In Language and Power, ed. Benedict R. O'G. Anderson. Ithaca: Cornell University Press.

Beidelman, T. O. 1993. *Moral Imagination in Kaguru Modes of Thought.* Washington, DC: Smithsonian Institution Press.

Benedict, Ruth. 1934. *Patterns of Culture.* New York: Houghton Mifflin.

Berry, Thomas Mary. 1999. *The Great Work,* 1st ed. New York: Bell Tower.

Douglas, Mary. 1978. *Cultural Bias.* London: Royal Anthropological Institute.

Fagg, Donald Ross. 1958. Authority and Social Stratification: A Study in Javanese Bureaucracy. PhD diss., Harvard University.

Geertz, Clifford. 1956. *The Development of the Javanese Economy: A Socio-Cultural Approach.* Cambridge, MA: Center for International Studies, Massachusetts Institute of Technology.

———. 1960. *The Religion of Java.* Glencoe, IL: Free Press.

———. 1963. *Agricultural Involution: The Process of Ecological Change in Indonesia.* Berkeley: Published for the Association of Asian Studies by University of California Press.

———. 1963. *Peddlers and Princes: Social Change and Economic Modernization in Two Indonesian Towns.* Chicago: University of Chicago Press.

———. 1965. *The Social History of an Indonesian Town.* Cambridge: MIT Press.

———. 1968. *Islam Observed.* New Haven: Yale University Press.

———. 1972. Deep Play: Notes on the Balinese Cockfight. *Daedalus* 101: 1–37.

———. 1973. *The Interpretation of Cultures.* New York: Basic Books.

———. 1980. *Negara: The Theatre State in Nineteenth-Century Bali.* Princeton: Princeton University Press.

———. 1983. *Local Knowledge.* New York: Basic Books.

———. 1995. *After the Fact: Two Countries, Four Decades, One Anthropologist.* Cambridge: Harvard University Press.

———. 1999. A Life of Learning. Charles Homer Haskins Lecture for 1999. New York: American Council of Learned Societies.

———. 2000. *Available Light: Anthropological Reflections on Philosophical Topics.* Princeton: Princeton University Press.

Goodenough, Ward. 1956. Residence Rules. *Southwestern Journal of Anthropology* 12.

———. 1967. Componential Analysis. *Science* 156.

Kroeber, Alfred. 1944. *Configurations of Cultural Growth.* Berkeley: University of California Press.

Kroeber, Alfred, and Clyde Kluckhohn. 1952. Culture: A Critical Review of Concepts and Definitions. *Peabody Museum Papers* 47, no. 1. Cambridge, MA: Peabody Museum.

Leach, Edmund. 1954. *Political Systems of Highland Burma.* Cambridge: Harvard University Press.

———. 1976. *Culture and Communication.* New York: Cambridge University Press.

Lévi-Strauss, Claude. [1955]. The Structural Study of Myth. *Journal of American Folklore* 68, no. 270: 428–44.

Mead, Margaret. 1953. National Character. In *Anthropology Today,* ed. A. L. Kroeber. Chicago: University of Chicago Press.

Middleton, John. 1960. *Lugbara Religion.* London: Oxford University.

Ortner, Sherry B. 1999. *The Fate of "Culture."* Berkeley: University of California Press.

Parsons, Talcott. 1961. *Theories of Society.* New York: Free Press of Glencoe.

Patterson, Thomas. 2001. *A Social History of Anthropology in the United States.* Oxford: Berg.

Peacock, James L. 1962. Pasamah Megaliths: Historical, Functional, and Conceptual Interpretations. *Academica Sinica* 13: 52–63.

———. 1968. *Rites of Modernization: Symbolic and Social Aspects of Indonesian Proletarian Drama.* Chicago: University of Chicago Press.

———. 1969. Mystics and Merchants in Fourteenth Century Germany: A Reconstruction of Their Psychological Bond and Its Implications for Social Change. *Journal for the Scientific Study of Religion* 3, no. 1: 47–59.

———. 1981. The Third Stream: Weber, Parsons, Geertz. *Journal of the Anthropological Society of Oxford* 12, no. 2: 122–29.

Pollock, Griselda. 1988. *Vision and Difference.* London: Routledge.

Schafer, D. Paul. 1998. *Culture: Beacon of the Future.* Westport, CT: Praeger.

Schneider, David M. 1968. *American Kinship.* Chicago: University of Chicago Department of Anthropology.

Turner, Victor. 1957. *Schism and Continuity in an African Society.* Northern Rhodesia: Manchester University Press.

Weber, Max. 1958. *The Religion of India.* Trans. and ed. Hans H. Gerth and Don Martindale. Glencoe, IL: Free Press.

Wikan, Unni. 1990. *Managing Turbulent Hearts.* Chicago: University of Chicago Press.

———. 1998. Culture—A New Concept of Race? Lessons from Norway. *Social Anthropology* 7, no. 1: 57–64.

Clifford Geertz and Islam

I N *AFTER BABEL,* George Steiner (1975, 24) observes that a "text is embedded in specific historical time," so that reading a text fully involves restoring "all that time can of the immediacies of value and intent in which speech actually occurs." This essay seeks to restore how the work of Clifford Geertz was initially read and heard in Islamic studies in the 1960s and 1970s—and indicate its contemporary significance for understanding Islam today.

KNOWING ISLAM AND ANTHROPOLOGY

Most of us learn the history of academic disciplines from when we enter the field, not from their beginnings (Ortner 1984). I entered two fields in the 1960s, Islamic studies and anthropology. From 1964 to 1966, I studied at the Institute for Islamic Studies at Montreal's McGill University, focusing on classical Arabic and developing a special interest in Islam and opposition to it in seventh-century Arabia (Eickelman 1967). Survey courses at McGill, the Castor Oil of graduate studies everywhere, covered the foundation texts of Islam and Islamic history. The name "Geertz" at the time passed the lips neither of mentors nor students, even in advanced seminars. Although several classmates at McGill were Indonesian, my lecture notes for those two years show virtually no reference to Islam in Southeast Asia. Unusual for survey courses on Islam in the1960s, McGill's balanced Islam and Islamic history in the Middle East with South Asia.

When I entered the University of Chicago's Department of Anthropology in September 1966, Bernard Cohn and Clifford Geertz taught that year's introductory "brainwashing" course—to use the student language of the time. Their complementary approaches were ideal. Cohn's course, which came in the fall, offered us the double vision of a professional historian and anthropologist. As in most introductory courses, the bulk of our readings were excerpts from a variety of different texts, but with Cohn they became more than an assemblage of "found" objects in the style of

Marcel Duchamp or a collation of predecessor's texts carefully chosen to persuade class participants of the inevitability of the lecturer's views—a form of pedagogical authority (Bourdieu and Passeron 1977) familiar to generations of graduate students.

Sartre aphoristically calls history "the deliberate resumption of the past by the present" (1962, 206). This phrase, which I had not yet encountered in 1968, perfectly conveys the consciousness of historiography and the historical imagination integral to Cohn's sense of "doing" history. At a measured pace he did more than convey a sense of anthropology's past. Anthropologists do not just "see" societies, they learn to see them at certain times in particular institutional settings.

Such a consciousness of "ways of knowing," elementary from the vantage of today, was innovative at a time when Chicago's Department of Anthropology, like most departments elsewhere, offered no courses in fieldwork. Students themselves organized an informal seminar in 1968, well before the tidal wave of reflexivity hit the discipline. We gleaned what we could from cryptic notes in the introductions of the classic ethnographies of the time and the occasional anecdotes conveyed by our mentors. Cohn's lectures invited us to pay equal attention to what anthropologists saw, experienced, and heard, and how—and to which audiences—they reported, wrote, and talked. His representation of the discipline's past conveyed a critical sense of how our own approach to "ways of knowing" influenced how we read the texts of our predecessors and contemporaries.

Geertz's pace and style of initiating us into anthropology in winter 1967 could not have differed more from Cohn's. What Evelyn Woods was to speed-reading, Clifford Geertz was to speed-speaking. Limited in size of note-taking group by the pressure of ballpoint pens on carbon paper, I worked in relay with two other students to record what we could of Geertz's rapid-fire lectures, tracing the notion of culture from figures such as Johann Herder, Wilhelm Dilthey, and Matthew Arnold to the 1960s. The names and texts flew hard and fast, although we later invoked them, half-digested and on the fly but sometimes appropriately, in comprehensive examinations. More immediately apprehended was the impression of Geertz caught in the act of trying to break out of the "iron cage" of received social thought. At the very least, Geertz made us acutely aware of the irregularities and shortcomings of anthropology as received tradition and practice. As our readings caught up with our excitement for the discipline, and as Geertz himself acknowledged, his sense of the emergence of a theory of culture was heavily filtered through the sieve of Harvard's Department of Social Relations, site of his own anthropological initiation beginning in 1950.

GEERTZ ON ISLAM IN THE 1960S AND 1970S

Geertz said almost nothing of Islam or of Indonesia in his formal "core" lectures in winter 1967, notwithstanding his intense and recent field research in Indonesia. It was discussed only in that year's oversubscribed advanced seminars. My first intimation of his approach to Indonesia came in a short required reading for Cohn's initiatory course, "Ritual and Social Change: A Javanese Example" (Geertz 1957), an article that captured our imaginations. It took the dominant theoretical conceptions of anthropology's immediate predecessors and sharpened our critical awareness of forms of social integration not allowed by so-called static functionalism—labeling any predecessor organizing concept as "static" was a fairly obvious cue that it was, or ought to be, on its way out.

The Hungarian composer György Ligeti (lecture, Wissenschaftskolleg zu Berlin, February 13, 2001) said of composing music that originality grows at the margins of the incessant repetition of the familiar. The same might be said of anthropology. Geertz, building on a distinction made by Pitirim A. Sorokin, one of his teachers at Harvard, distinguished between "logico-meaningful," or cultural, integration—"a unity of style, of logical implication, of meaning and value"—and "causal functional," or social system integration—the kind "one finds in an organism," with each part an element in a "reverberating causal ring" (Geertz 1957, 34). Geertz argued that distinguishing between these two forms of social integration (and adding the element of individual motivation), better accounted for the "interference"—Geertz's term—of political with religious meanings and the "open struggle for power" in Javanese village society. Geertz's argument reassuringly used elements of the social theory we were then learning, but also offered a way beyond the conventional ideas of the day, even if he still called it a "dynamic functionalist approach" (34). We saw the article as a model for breaking into mainstream anthropological journals. It showed how the modification of an existing anthropological approach could improve the questions asked and the answers given. Edmund Leach's *Political Systems of Highland Burma* (1954), in retrospect also a creative break with conventional structural-functional anthropology, was also part of our core readings. It addressed issues of social change but offered no direct development of the idea of culture. Geertz's approach intrigued us more because it encompassed a renewed attention to the idea of culture as well as that of the dynamics of societal change.

Like my fellow students in 1967–68, I was almost exclusively concerned with the theoretical implications of Geertz's argument, not its implications for the study of Islam in particular or religion in general. Nonetheless, eager to relate anthropology as a discipline to understanding Islam, I chose Geertz's *The Religion of Java* (1960) as an optional reading for a timed essay in Cohn's initiation course. *Religion of Java* exemplifies full-strength thick description. Prior to coming to Chicago in 1966, I was immersed for two years in what Marshall Hodgson, Chicago's leading scholar on Islam until his sudden death in 1968, referred to as this high culture. Hodgson's focus was the dynamics of religious debate and change in Islamic "high" culture. He acknowledged that the traditions of "peasants or even non-lettered people" had their own dynamics of change, but he explicitly left aside any detailed discussion of such change or how transformations in peasant and high culture might have been interrelated or even share common background understandings (Hodgson 1974, I: 80). For a student with a certain amount of "Islamic" learning but only a tentative grasp of social theory, *Religion of Java* was particularly appealing because it related the vicissitudes of "high" Islamic culture in Java with the rest of society, including what Geertz (1957, 49) called the "more or less" fully urbanized elite, the "more or less traditionally organized peasantry," and all the fluctuating in-between social forms. Even in his earliest writing, Geertz's complex qualifications and self-conscious prose invited readers to think on two related levels. Geertz's ethnographic reporting can never be reduced to the Jack Webb (of "Dragnet" fame) approach of "just the facts, ma'am." It also called attention to the frailty and uncertainty of even the best of ethnographic reporting and analysis.

Religion contains an implicit set of theoretical assumptions concerning how adequately to represent the religion of a complex religious tradition—Islam in this case—not limited to a single regional or national setting. For scholars of Islam, *Religion* suggested how anthropologists and others could apply what was learned from the study of the religious words and deeds of small-scale groups or communities to larger entities, including nations and historical traditions. Geertz divided Javanese religious practices into the three now-familiar "orientations" or "cultural types": *abangan,* associated in a "broad and general" way with Javanese villagers; *santri,* a "purer Islam" associated in a "broad and general" way with Javanese traders in villages and towns; and a Hindu-Javanese *prijaji* tradition associated with the hereditary aristocracy (Geertz 1960, 5–6). Geertz argued that these three subtraditions refracted an underlying cultural unity, so that, for example, the *prijaji* and *abangan* cultural orientations were "in part but genteel and vulgar versions of one another" (234).

All the qualifications and cautions in Geertz's narrative called painful attention to the fragility of social theory and ethnographic practice. The "in part" and "more or less" cautions embedded in the above quotations to relate particular religious "subtraditions" to particular social categories suggest an unambiguous awareness of the difficulties involved in adequately representing the various "strands" of Javanese religious practice and belief in cultural theory as it had developed through the early 1960s. The title of the book itself, as opposed to alternative possibilities such as *Islam in Java,* which could have been a parallel to Robert Bellah's *Tokugawa Religion* (1957), represented an implicit choice in how to represent Javanese religious experience.

Geertz (personal communication, November 23, 2002) preferred the title *Religions of Java,* but the publisher's insistence on religion in the singular won the day and perhaps better reflects the book's overall strategy. After all, the book concludes, perhaps with intended irony that the holiday of *rijaja* is "a kind of master symbol for Javanese culture, as perhaps Christmas is for ours," and that if one understood "everything" concerning *rijaja,* "a simple impossibility—one could say one understood the Javanese"(Geertz 1960, 379).

This passage is vintage Geertz. It can be read at face value. Or it can be read as deliberately combining ironies and paradoxes, like those present in Jorge Luis Borges's short story, "El Aleph," in which the narrator discovers in a dark corner of a friend's cellar "one of those points of space that contains all other spaces" (Borges 1962, 186, author's translation), and through which one can at once see all things past and present. Whether Geertz's comparison of *rijaja* with Christmas is intended at face value or as end-of-book humor emanating from the furious pace—six uninterrupted months of writing in an office at the Massachusetts Institute of Technology, he once said—matters less than his reminder to readers of the complexities of writing ethnography in an era when the "it is written" style of ethnography ("The Kaguru assume . . .") still prevailed.

Geertz's first book to deal explicitly with Islam as world religious tradition, *Islam Observed* (1968a), based on the Terry lectures given a year earlier at Yale University, remains good to think with. For its original audience, the book broke with the history of religions and Islamic studies traditions of looking for single, unifying religious essences and instead considered the implications of strongly contrasting ethnographic and historical characterizations of the Islamic tradition as it unfolded at the antipodes of the Muslim majority world, Indonesia and Morocco.

Islam Observed offered to its original audience two major conceptual innovations to the comparative study of religions and to the writing of anthropology for audiences well beyond its specialist base. The dominant trend in the history of religions through the 1960s was a reliance on typological classifications of phenomena being compared, such as "mysticism," that presumed in advance the "essential" features of the phenomena being considered. In focusing on the particular, displayed through vivid characterizations of the representations and practices of Moroccan and Javanese saints in their respective social and historical contexts, Geertz suggested an alternative strategy based on "family resemblances"—partial similarities that can be compared and contrasted rather than slotted into taxonomies. Geertz imported this concept into anthropology from the post-analytic philosophy of Ludwig Wittgenstein, just as he also introduced Alfred Schutz's (1967, 15) distinctions among predecessors, consociates, contemporaries, and successors, distinctions that became commonplace in anthropology after the publication of *Person, Time, and Conduct in Bali* (Geertz 1966a). By importing such concepts to anthropology, Geertz joined the field more forcefully with wider currents in social thought, making anthropology more visible, and vital, to a large public. His approach also suggested to others ways of following parallel paths. It influenced my work on the changing role of religious intellectuals and ideas of learning in Muslim societies (Eickelman 1985).

Geertz's second major contribution was to close the practical gap in academic training and styles of writing between anthropology and history (see Cohn 1980, 1981). *Islam Observed* "more or less"—to employ the common Geertzian phrase—conveys the different historical contexts in which the dominant "classical" styles of Islamic expression and practice developed in Morocco and Indonesia. Elements of his argument have been superseded, as historian of religion Vincent Cornell (1998) argues for Morocco in *Realm of the Saint,* a study of religious experience in fifteenth- and sixteenth-century Morocco that also situates Moroccan Sufism in the context of comparable developments elsewhere in the Middle East and in Christian Europe (see also Munson 1993 for Morocco; for Java, see Woodward 1989). Geertz articulated changing and contested ideas of culture with what happened in history, prompting others to essay better arguments.

In *Islam Observed* as in his other writings, Geertz's consistent goal was to develop an improved concept of culture (Eickelman interview with Clifford Geertz, CBS-TV "Sunrise Semester," November 26, 1974). At times, his arresting metaphors and images hyperbolically overreach, as in the comparison between the Javanese *rijaja* and Christmas. Thus *Islam*

Observed concludes with what Geertz calls a "human metaphor" of a traditionally raised French-speaking Moroccan student on an airplane bound for New York, his first trip outside of Morocco, passing "the entire trip with the Koran gripped in one hand and a glass of Scotch in the other" (Geertz 1968, 116–17)—quite a feat for a six-hour flight. But such flopped images are rare. Accompanying Geertz's major essays of the period was a steady stream of reviews and review essays such as "Mysteries of Islam" (1975a), a review of Marshall Hodgson's *Venture of Islam,* "Conjuring with Islam" (1982), and a variety of single-book reviews that brought specialist studies of Islam to the ken of a wider public and encouraged specialists from several fields to reach across conventional disciplinary boundaries.

Geertz's work on Islam is inseparable from the wider goal of significantly developing the concept of culture from earlier anthropological uses of the term and making the newer use of the term an integral part of modern social thought—the lynchpin of virtually all of his essays, not just the "as a cultural system" series that encompassed ideology (1964), religion (1966b), common sense (1975b) and art (1976). Essays introducing a wide public to the cultural implications of Moroccan naming practices (1975c) and comparing the royal progress in Elizabethan England with Mulay Hasan I's in late-nineteenth-century Morocco (1977) convey specific manifestations of the idea of culture to a wide audience. Most pertinent to the study of Islam—and the understanding of economics "as a cultural system"—is "Suq: The Bazaar Economy in Sefrou, Morocco" (1979), a major and heavily empirical book-length essay with a deceptively modest title, a data-laden essay showing the practical articulation of religious ideologies and institutions with politics and specific social classes and groups.

One would like to think that the argument for a concept of culture that is contested, contingent, and emerging—a notion that Geertz has done so much to convey to a wider public—would have displaced earlier, and in retrospect impoverished, notions of cultures and civilizations as fairly fixed entities. Yet Samuel Huntington's notion of "West vs. the Rest," in which "Islam" and "Confucianism" are pitted against the "West" (1993), relies heavily on the ideas of Arnold Toynbee's (1947) moralizing and historical stereotypy rather than newer ideas of culture that emphasize the incessant crossing and constructed nature of civilizational and cultural boundaries. Some of Geertz's characterizations of culture, such as comparing it to an octopus (1966, 67–68) with its "partial integrations, partial incongruencies, and partial independencies" were geared primarily to specialists in the anthropological trade. Other essays were meant for a wider public, such as the1983 Huxley Memorial Lecture, which contains an element of conceptual evangelism to those who would support quantitative approaches to the exclusion of others: "The setting aside of cultural factors altogether as something for Islamologists, mythographers, and shadow-play enthusiasts to deal with seems to lead not to increased precision but to ascending indeterminacy" (Geertz 1989, 523).

THINKING AS A MORAL ACT: GEERTZ'S IMPACT TODAY

There are several enduring contributions of Geertz's life and work to the study of Islam. First, he recognized the continuing role of religion and religious debates in modern societies. Resistance to the idea of culture was not confined to quantitative positivists. In "Marabouts in the Market-Place," in part a review of *Moroccan Islam* (Eickelman 1976), the late Ernest Gellner (1981, 218) issued a strong rebuke against the use of "cloud-culture-talk" derived from the "school" of Clifford Geertz. The reduction of Geertz to "cloud-culture-talk" is difficult to reconcile with Geertz (1972), which brings the arguments of *Religion in Java* up to date and rereads them in the wake of the murderous violence that followed Indonesia's 1965 coup d'état and the subsequent purges of "communists" that by some accounts left as many as half a million dead and hundreds of thousands more in prison. Against this backdrop, Geertz argued that the most salient religious development in Indonesia since midcentury was the "hesitant" emergence of "something rather like a denominational pattern of religious organization or affiliation," and toward a "more openly pluralistic system" (1972, 70–71), if not always a tolerant one, and one in which cultural understandings shaped, and were shaped by, the social and political contexts in which they took place.

This short 1972 article demonstrates more than the continuing significance of Geertz's earlier interpretations and their relevance to dramatically changed social circumstances. On rereading Geertz's earliest work on religion in Indonesia, especially in light of the views about the inevitability of secularization prevalent in the 1950s and 1960s, Geertz insisted that religion as idea and practice still mattered. The secular bias of modernization theory has had a significant role in deflecting attention away from the continued role of religious practices and values in contemporary societies, including the Muslim majority world.

Geertz sensed this continuing importance of religious thought and action to modern society while other influential thinkers accepted with few qualifications the assumption that religion and religious intellectuals, who earlier played central societal roles, were doomed to play increasingly marginal ones in modern and "modernizing" societies (Shils 1972, 17). In the bold language of Daniel Lerner, the Muslim world faced the stark choice of "Mecca or mechanization" (1964, 405), a bleak view echoed by Manfred Halperin, who saw the Muslim world as faced with the unpalatable choice between a "neo-Islamic totalitarianism" intent on "resurrecting the past" or a "reformist Islam" that would open "the sluice gates and [be] swamped by the deluge" (1963, 129). For Geertz, in contrast, the role of religion, like that of ethnic identities, was dynamic and evolving rather than primordial and fixed. These powerful ideas are, of course, echoed in the work of successors to Geertz on the role of Islam in Indonesia, including Robert Hefner (1985, 2000) and John Bowen (1993; 2003).

Second, "Ritual and Social Change," like *Religion in Java,* boldly captured religious debates that were permeating villages as vigorously as urban life. It was not only in major urban centers that ideas and debates over religious practice had a strong resonance but also in villages and small towns. Throughout the Muslim world most scholars emphasized developments in major urban centers and religious institutions—a trend fully in accord with the self-image of traditionally educated religious scholars ('*ulama*) throughout the Muslim majority world as the "guardians" of faith and religious tradition. Like other mortals, Geertz has not always made the right calls in inferring long-term trends, as when he wrote that the Javanese were turning "toward a more experiential sort of faith, and especially toward mysticism" and "a personal, inward, transcendental experience" (1972, 72–73). Here Geertz got it half right—more than most of us manage—in that two major developments in Java's "experiential turn" have been the development of a strong nationwide movement of moderate, educated Muslims as a major political force (Hefner 2000), the underside of which has been a smaller but deadly movement of extremist violence among groups such as the Laskar Jihad (Hefner 2003).

In Indonesia and elsewhere, mass higher education, mass communications, new media, and the greater ease of travel has facilitated the fragmentation of political and religious authority and the development of new voices that contest or ignore established authority (Eickelman and Piscatori 1996, 121–35). Accompanying these developments has been the objectification of religious knowledge in the form of explicit questions such as "What is my religion?" "Why is it important to my life?" and "How do my beliefs guide my conduct?" (Eickelman 1992). This refiguring of practice and the religious imagination is as important at the village level as in towns, in Indonesia (Bowen 1993) as in Pakistan (Marsden 2003). What Geertz got absolutely right from the very beginning of his field research was the centrality of talk and religious practice and the role of ideas at all social levels and contexts. Again, an early statement of Geertz's awareness of the importance of ideas is his "Thinking as a Moral Act: Ethical Dimensions of Anthropological Fieldwork in the New States" (1968b). Geertz narrates how he often loaned his typewriter to a local poet, until one day he asked for its return in a way that implied to the poet that his work was less important than the anthropologist's own. Geertz's rapport with the poet was never restored, but the subtext again affirms the importance of local knowledge and practice and its role in shaping wider social and cultural currents.

Finally, Geertz has—with a few exceptions such as Huntington—infused a newer and more persuasive notion of culture into the wider framework of social thought. Anthropologists earlier thought of their academic discipline as the one most involved with the concept of culture, but the concept has, so to speak, lost its anthropological copyright and has developed in multiple ways in fields such as cultural studies. Geertz's work has pervaded studies of Islam and thinking about religion. In his work on the cult of the saints in early Latin Christianity, Peter Brown (1981, 9–10) acknowledges how writing on contemporary Moroccan religiosity has stimulated his approach to a much earlier era. Explicit discussion of culture occurs only at the margins of Vincent Cornell's historical study of Moroccan Sufism (for example, 1998, 61–62, 155–56), but a dialogue with Geertz and others who have characterized Moroccan religiosity permeates Cornell's approach.

The first teaching post of one of anthropology's distinguished predecessors, Edward Evans-Pritchard (1902–1973), was at Cairo's Fuad I University (now the University of Cairo) in the early 1930s. He spoke Arabic and conducted field research in Egypt's western desert before deciding to conduct field research among the Nuer of the southern Sudan. Anthropology's oral history (author's interview with Robert Fernea, CBS-TV "Sunrise Semester," October 23, 1974) has it that "E-P" decided not to make his career in the Arab world because of the need to work among scholars of other disciplines. Nuer society offered a prime exemplar of an "elementary" society more in line with the anthropological expectations of the era.

Geertz's approach could not be more different. In Indonesia as in Morocco his work plunged him into contexts where anthropologists could never claim an exclusive interpretive role. In the irony that characterized many of his hypertextual commentaries on the practice of anthropology and the study of Islam, Geertz (personal communication, 1973) once suggested only to ask questions that could be answered. Fortunately, Geertz rarely follows his own advice. Neither his questions nor the answers offered in his essays—his preferred narrative form—provide a sense of completion, reminding us that no ethnographic essay can. *Islam Observed,* for example, incorporated an intensive reading of "secondary" literature on Morocco in French and English; his major field research in Morocco was still underway. Yet the questions posed have helped shape thinking about religion in the modern world as few other texts have managed to do (for example, Casanova 1994). Geertz's work in Indonesia, as in Morocco, breaks away from conventional disciplinary boundaries. For Islamic studies, Geertz's work suggests how historians, anthropologists, and scholars in other disciplines can place their work in thick description ethnographic context—and still communicate to wider publics. Geertz has posed questions that matter, and his answers, with their "partial integrations, partial incongruencies, and partial independencies," remain good to think with. Qualifications such as "more or less" and "partial" are invitations to thought, and this is Geertz's major contribution to understanding Islam and to anthropology.

ACKNOWLEDGMENTS

I am grateful to Jon W. Anderson and Brian Didier for comments on an earlier version of this essay.

REFERENCES

Bellah, Robert N. 1957. *Tokugawa Religion: The Values of Pre-Industrial Japan.* Boston: Beacon Press.

Borges, Jorge Luis. 1962. *El Aleph.* Buenos Aires: Emecé Editores.

Bourdieu, Pierre, and Jean-Claude Passeron, 1977. *Reproduction in Education, Society and Culture.* Beverly Hills, CA: Sage.

Bowen, John R. 1993. *Muslims through Discourse: Religion and Ritual in Gayo Society.* Princeton: Princeton University Press.

———. 2003. *Islam, Law, and Equality in Indonesia: An Anthropology of Public Reasoning.* Cambridge: Cambridge University Press.

Brown, Peter. 1981. *The Cult of the Saints: Its Rise and Function in Latin Christianity.* Chicago: University of Chicago Press.

Casanova, José. 1994. *Public Religions in the Modern World.* Chicago: University of Chicago Press.

Cohn, Bernard S. 1980. History and Anthropology: The State of Play. *Comparative Studies in Society and History* 22, no. 2 (April): 198–221.

———. 1981. Anthropology and History in the 1980s. *Journal of Interdisciplinary History* 12, no. 2 (Autumn): 227–52.

Cornell, Vincent J. 1998. *Realm of the Saint: Power and Authority in Moroccan Sufism.* Austin: University of Texas Press.

Eickelman, Dale F. 1967. Musaylima: An Approach to the Social Anthropology of Seventh Century Arabia. *Journal of the Social and Economic History of the Orient* 10, no. 1: 17–52.

———. 1976. *Moroccan Islam: Tradition and Society in a Pilgrimage Center.* Austin: University of Texas Press.

———. 1985. *Knowledge and Power in Morocco: The Education of a Twentieth-Century Notable.* Princeton: Princeton University Press.

———. 1992. Mass Higher Education and the Religious Imagination in Contemporary Arab Societies. *American Ethnologist* 19, no. 4 (November): 1–13.

Eickelman, Dale F., and James Piscatori. 1996. *Muslim Politics.* Princeton: Princeton University Press.

Geertz, Clifford. 1957. Ritual and Social Change: A Javanese Example. *American Anthropologist* 59, no. 1 (February): 32–54.

———. 1960. *The Religion of Java.* New York: Free Press of Glencoe.

———. 1964. Ideology as a Cultural System, 47–76. In *Ideology and Discontent,* ed. David Apter. New York: Free Press.

———. 1966a. *Person, Time, and Conduct in Bali: An Essay in Cultural Analysis.* New Haven: Yale University Southeast Asia Studies.

———. 1966b. Religion as a Cultural System, 1–46. In *Anthropological Approaches to the Study of Religion,* ed. Michael Banton. London: Tavistock.

———. 1968a. *Islam Observed: Religious Development in Morocco and Indonesia.* New Haven: Yale University Press.

———. 1968b. Thinking as a Moral Act: Ethical Dimensions of Fieldwork in the New States. *Antioch Review* 27: 134–59.

———. 1972. Religious Change and Social Order in Soeharto's Indonesia. *Asia* 27, no. 3 (Autumn): 62–84.

———. 1975a. Mysteries of Islam. *New York Review of Books* 22, no. 20 (December 11): 18–26.

———. 1975b. Common Sense as a Cultural System. *Antioch Review* 33: 47–53.

———. 1975c. On the Nature of Anthropological Understanding. *American Scientist* 63, no. 1 (January–February): 47–53.

———. 1976. Art as a Cultural System. *Modern Language Notes* 91: 1473–99.

———. 1977. Centers, Kings, and Charisma: Reflections on the Symbolics of Power, 150–71. In *Culture and Its Creators: Essays in Honor of Edward Shils,* ed. Joseph Ben-David and Terry N. Clark. Chicago: University of Chicago Press.

———. 1978. Suq: The Bazaar Economy in Sefrou, 159–268. In *Meaning and Order in Moroccan Society,* ed. Clifford Geertz, Hildred Geertz, and Lawrence Rosen. New York: Cambridge University Press.

———. 1982. Conjuring with Islam. *New York Review of Books* 29 (May 27): 25–28.

Gellner, Ernest. [1977] 1981. Marabouts in the Market-Place. In *Muslim Society.* Cambridge: Cambridge University Press.

Halperin, Manfred. 1962. *The Politics of Social Change in the Middle East and North Africa.* Princeton: Princeton University Press.

Hefner, Robert W. 1985. *Hindu Javanese: Tengger Tradition and Islam.* Princeton: Princeton University Press.

―――. 2000. *Civil Islam: Muslims and Democratization in Indonesia.* Princeton: Princeton University Press.

―――. 2003. Civic Pluralism Denied? *Jihadi* Radicals and New Media in Post-Suharto Indonesia," 158–79. In *New Media in the Muslim World: The Emerging Public Sphere,* ed. Dale F. Eickelman and Jon W. Anderson. Bloomington: Indiana University Press.

Marshall Hodgson. 1974. *The Venture of Islam: Conscience and History in a World Civilization,* 3 vols. Chicago: University of Chicago Press.

Huntington, Samuel P. 1993. The Clash of Civilizations? *Foreign Affairs* 72, no. 3 (Summer): 22–49.

Leach, Edmund. 1954. *The Political Systems of Highland Burma.* Boston: Beacon.

Lerner, Daniel. [1958] 1964. *The Passing of Traditional Society: Modernizing the Middle East.* New York: Free Press.

Marsden, Magnus. 2003. Islamization and Globalization in Chitral, Northern Pakistan. PhD diss., Department of Social Anthropology, University of Cambridge.

Munson, Henry, Jr. 1993. *Religion and Power in Morocco.* New Haven: Yale University Press.

Ortner, Sherry B. 1984. Theory in Anthropology since the Sixties. *Comparative Studies in Society and History* 26, no. 1 (January): 126–66.

Sartre, Jean-Paul. 1962. *Literary and Philosophic Essays.* New York: Collier.

Schutz, Alfred. 1967. *Collected Papers, vol. I: The Problem of Social Reality,* ed. Maurice Natanson. The Hague: Martinus Nijhoff.

Shils, Edward. 1975. *The Intellectuals and the Powers and Other Essays.* Chicago: University of Chicago Press.

Steiner, George. 1975. *After Babel: Aspects of Language and Translation.* New York: Oxford University Press.

Toynbee, Arnold J. 1947. *A Study of History,* abridged by D. C. Sommervell. New York: Oxford University Press.

Woodward, Mark R. 1989. *Islam in Java: Normative Piety and Mysticism in the Sultanate of Yogyakarta.* Tucson: University of Arizona Press.

Deep Play, Violence, and
Social Reconstruction

F OR CLIFFORD GEERTZ: Errant Thoughts in a Blurred Genre—
Errant—but hopefully not too erring. Thoughts in a blurred genre.
Between the *Festschrift*—in which one offers in tribute one's own work as
an extension of one's teacher's work—and the *slide show* on "works and
lives." Indeed two slides can serve as frames: a slide of a fabulous large
tapestry of a fighting cock that hangs in one of the chemical engineering
buildings at MIT, a locus to which I shall return; and a slide of a painting
of a buzkashi game that I recently brought back from Central Asia and
that now hangs in my house, a game to which I shall also return.

So: errant thoughts in a blurred genre—for Clifford Geertz—in three
movements: where we are now, where we have been, and on the trail
of an anthropology to come. (One of the condundra of trying to talk
about Cliff's work is that the very language of anthropology—the prose
we speak—is suffused with the metaphors he has taught us to think with:
turtles and metaphors all the way down.)

PART ONE: WHERE WE ARE NOW
Emergent Forms of Life and the Anthropological Voice;
OR:
A post-Geertzian manifesto, where "post," "posts," and "postings"
are defined as a sending-receiving relation
between fathers and sons,
and between the three or four phases of self-defined Geertzian work.

I start with an ethnographic datum, a stance toward ethics and politics,
and a contextualist stance toward social theory.

We live (again) in an era in which there is a pervasive claim, or native
model, asserted by practitioners in many contemporary arenas of life (law,
sciences, political economy, computer technologies, education, etc.) that
traditional concepts and ways of doing things no longer work, that life
is outrunning the pedagogies in which we were trained, that we are ex-
periencing emergent new forms of life—in new cyborgian, hybrid, cross-

species biotechnological forms of life, in databank-networked and new materials infrastructures, in environmental and ecological changes, and in the legal, economic, psychological, and social institutional innovations that these require. *Call this native model an ethnographic datum.*

We live therefore (again) in an era in which new ethical and political spaces are thrown up that require action and can often have quite serious consequences, but for which the possibilities for giving grounds quickly run out. Traditional ethical and moral guides seem not always helpful, and we are often left to negotiate interests and trade-offs in legal or other tournaments of decision-making over time, and across terrains configured with multiply interacting new technologies, what I call ethical plateaus with due deference to Giles Deleuze, Gregory Bateson, and the Balinese. *Call this a philosophical stance toward ethics and politics,* one that Ludwig Wittgenstein formulated when he said that giving grounds comes to an end somewhere and that "the end is not an ungrounded presupposition; it is an ungrounded way of acting" or a "form of life," a sociality of action that always already contains within it ethical dilemmas, or, in the idiom of Emmanuel Levinas, "the face of the other." The "face of the other" is particularly of concern in the peopling of new technologies and technosciences.

In coming to terms with this ethnographic datum and this philosophical stance, anthropology is pushed to develop new tools of social theory. The social theory of the last quarter of the twentieth century and beginning of the twenty-first is created out of quite different generational, social structural, communication infrastructural, and knowledge-making contexts and experiences from those out of which classical social theory was created at the end of the nineteenth century and turn of the twentieth. *Call this a contextualist stance toward social and cultural theory.* Classical social theory is hardly passé or superseded, but Marx, Weber, Dilthey, Freud, Durkheim, Fleck, Mauss, Schutz, et al. did not experience or analyze the kinds of shifts that have become focal for post-Algerian independence French theory (Cixcous, Deleuze and Guattari, Foucault, Derrida, Lyotard, Baudrillard, Touraine, Abeles, Latour, et al.), post-Green movement theory in Germany (Ulrich Beck, Friedrich Kittler) and Italy (Agamben, Melucci), post-cost-benefit analysis of high hazard high consequence industries from anesthesiology to aeronautics to nuclear power in the United States (Perrow), post-socialist nationalisms, and, importantly for my own work, social and cultural movements in the Islamic world seeking to move beyond patriarchal patrimonialism (inspired among others by Ali Shariati, Nawal al-Sadawi, Saad Ibrahim; and the powerful films coming out of Iran). Indeed today—on the very day that NATO is being expanded, and that we are contemplating war in Iraq—we operate under the sign of the film *Safar-e Qandahar* by the Iranian director Mohsen Makhmalbaf, and its image of prostheses being parachuted from Red Cross helicopters to Afghan men running on crutches to catch them.

In the 1990s anthropology began to take up ethnographic challenges in a number of critical arenas: *work on the reconstruction of society* in the wake of social trauma, structural violence, and disruption on a scale not reflected upon, though it existed, by the social sciences since the early post–World War II, post-India-Pakistan Partition, and post-wars of decolonization era in which Clifford Geertz got his anthropological start. 1990s anthropology began to take up ethnographic *work on the new communication technologies* that mediate the contemporary analogues of what Durkheim might have called the conscience collective in their more differentiated, telemediated, transnationally diffuse guises, and *that transform the conditions of possibility for governance, legitimacy, and democratic civil societies*. And 1990s anthropology began to take up ethnographic *work on the infrastructures of what we make live and who we let die*.

To map and critique these technoscientific worlds and infrastructures, interferences and mediations, dislocations and reconfigurations, cultural forces and autoimmune cultural toxicities (CNN to al-Jazeera) requires an anthropology attentive to an expanding variety of cultural differences that go far beyond traditionally understood cultural differences. The distinctive anthropological voice—the aspiration for cross-culturally comparative, socially grounded, linguistically attentive perspectives—continues to be a valuable jewel among the social sciences amidst the pressures to simply turn to statistical indices for all policies and judgments.

Thus far the inconstant son's sendings to the father; let me turn to the generative sendings of the father to the son.

PART TWO: WHERE WE HAVE BEEN
Rethinking the Anthropology of the Second Half
of the Twentieth Century with Clifford Geertz;
OR:
Cliff's four phases and my three-fold epistemological interpretive grid.

In his most recent of three essays surveying his own "works and lives," Cliff uses a four-fold division. There is the golden age of optimistic post–World War II reconstruction, multidisciplinarity and team research, modernization and development theories grounded in Max Weber's notions of economic, political, and cultural rationalizations, and the voluntarism of Talcott Parsons's layer cake of biological, psychological, social, and cultural systems, the latter three, respectively, being dynamically integrated, functionally integrated, and logico-meaningfully integrated with cybernetic feedback among them, such that they were always already inseparable except analytically or heuristically. This was the age of Cliff's field-defining quartet of ethnographic monographs on Indonesia.

There followed the dramatic shift of the hot spots of the Cold War into Indonesia. Thus the silver age of his migration to Sefrou in Morocco, and the efforts of the Committee for the Comparative Study of New Nations at Chicago to keep the modernization theories going as they obviously splintered and decayed. His ethnography became less monographic, and justifications were found for turning to the essay form in *Local Knowledge,* and the tributes to such literary idols as Lionel Trilling. It is this turn that contains, I think, much of the ambivalence of his own corpus of work and its uneasy relation to the work of some of his progeny.

There followed the bronze and iron ages in anthropology of the 1980s and 1990s, which Cliff glosses as a florescence of different schools and isms in the social sciences, followed most recently by a return of "unclear significance" to concerns with violence, ethnic conflict, and the like. This is the period of blurred genres, Cliff's being in multiple minds about the role of Islam, and so on.

This is, however, the period, in my own trajectory and that of my cohort, of *Writing Culture, Anthropology as Cultural Critique, Debating Muslims,* the eight-volume *Late Editions Project,* the *Public Culture Project,* the inauguration of the journal *Cultural Anthropology,* my own directing of a Center for Cultural Studies, and then directing a Program in Science, Technology and Society. I count myself as one of Clifford Geertz's progeny, perhaps an inconstant disciple, nonetheless both a fan, and I hope an appreciative and constructive deployer of his insights. My own work followed along behind Cliff's early interest in ecology, his efforts to test Weberian accounts of sociologically stratified and differentially organized religious forms (in my case in the Caribbean, Iran, and India), his interest in the philosophy of the social sciences, in genres of literary and dramatic forms, and eventually in science and technology. And I particularly want to salute Cliff's repeated efforts to appoint a science studies person at the Institute for Advanced Studies.

I would divide Geertz's four phases into three epistemological ones. I think one of the most fascinating features of Clifford Geertz's writings is the shift from a comparativist Weberian, Parsonian, and broadly positivist or positive knowledge production, intended to help with notions of development programs for the modernization of "new nations" in old cultures and civilizations (a contradiction that soon became generative both descriptively and epistemologically). It is a shift from the rich ethnographic work of *Agricultural Involution, Religions in Java* as it's author titled it (not as it was titled in the singular by its publisher (Geertz, *After the Fact*, 1995 [hereafter AF], 55), *The Social History of an Indonesian Town, Peddlers and Princes,* and such essays as "Religion and Social Change," "Deep Play," and perhaps, but maybe not, "Person, Time, and Conduct in Bali,"[1] but certainly the later *Negara.* By the time we get to *After the Fact* and *Available Light* we are in the presence of an *ostad,* a master, of a very different kind of epistemology, one that plays deeply described cultures off against one another in a comparative epistemology, rather than a comparative realism, where as Geertz himself says, "One is faced with complex and contradictory fields of significative action, most of it tacit, across which assertion and denial, celebration and complaint, authority and resistance, continuously move." He is talking about comparing Indonesia and Morocco, and he continues, "When ingeniously juxtaposed, these fields can shed a certain amount of light on one another, but they are neither variants of one another nor expressions of some superfield that transcends them both" (AF, 49). I would call this *using the epistemological resources of one culture to critique and see anew into another culture.* In this example, Geertz is musing upon the lack of gender inflections in Javanese, and its minutely graded, hierarchical speech registers, in contrast to Moroccan Arabic, which "has gender inflections for just about every part of speech, but no status forms" (AF, 46). By so musing, he comes upon the insight—which he does not actually develop, though it would be fascinating to do so—that by looking at Moroccan politics with Javanese eyes (or grammars and speech modes), he is suddenly struck by the "persistent edge of seduction and resistance, flirtation and conquest . . . ranging from the understanding of sainthood to the metaphors of insult." Moroccan politics is a world of flirtation and seduction, "where rank and station are sexually charged."

Geertz in this most recent phase of his epistemological self-reflections speaks of this sort of comparative "method," or, since he eschews the term "method," artistic, even intuitive, skill, of these fields of "significative action, most of it tacit, across which assertion and denial, celebration and complaint, authority and resistance, continuously move"—as comparing incommensurables. Nonetheless, he concedes, it is "a useful enterprise, and when the stars are right, an informative one, however illogical."

Illogical? I would submit even in passing, that hermeneutics and performance are not illogical, either as method or as art, and that entertaining work in the comparative critical apparatuses of local hermeneutics is both methodical and reasonable, and at least culturally logical.

Geertz's middle passage, where I suppose the contradictions of the Parsonian vision, came to accumulate so many anomalies that a paradigm shift was needed and was found in the Geisteswissenschaften of Dilthey, Weber, and Schutz, the counter-canon to which we were treated by Cliff in the 1960s. (We also found our way to Hans-Georg Gadamer's *Truth and Method;* to Walter Benjamin and Theodor Adorno; and to Paul Ricoeur, Kenneth Burke, Victor Turner, and Mircea Eliade who were important presences for my cohort at Chicago—and even, very sotto voce at Chicago, Claude Lévi-Strauss read as talmud rather than as machine, Marx read as a decipherer of symbolic hieroglyphics of suffering and meaning as well as a political economist and a Saul Alinsky organizer *avant la lettre*). This middle passage was the time of the essays of the *Interpretation of Culture,* essays that we as graduate students were enthralled by, and tried without comparable success to mimic in our various term papers, mimicking the vocabulary, the bons mots, the paradoxes and chiasmuses, and elegant turns of polished phrase: models of/models for, experience near/experience far, many, as with all good poets, borrowed from, and gaining resonance from, the sedimented metaphors in the language and epistemological threads of earlier practitioners, Dilthey's *Vorbildt* und *Nachbildt,* Kohut's experience near and experience far, Gilbert Ryle's thick description and public language routing the ghosts in the machine, Paul Ricoeur's social action leaving traces that could be read as texts, Jeremy Bentham's deep play, Alfred Schutz's consociates. The middle passage was ethnographic as well as epistemological: Morocco did not yield up the monographic ethnographic treatments that Indonesia did, though *Islam Observed,* and *Meaning and Order in Moroccan Society* had their brilliant insights and verbal pointillisms such as the much quoted image of the mental compartmentalization used by the modern Muslim of undecidable piety on the airplane with Scotch in one hand and the Koran for safety in the other.

This is the middle passage from cultural systems, the era of the hegemony of linguistic models: structural linguistics, generative grammars, cybernetics, paradigms, structuralisms, and the efforts to reformat phenomenology into more systemic modes whether in Sartre's effort to fuse existentialism and marxism or the socialization of perception through cultural forms, cockfights, calendars, teknonymic kinship namings, ethnosemantics, religion as a cultural system, models of/models for, common sense as a cultural system, art as a cultural system, ideology as a cultural system. The middle passage is from these recursive, self-protective symbolic systems to interpretive modes of blurred genres, incommensurable fields of significative action, reading over one another's shoulders, and like a moiré flitting back and forth between narrative local worlds and world-historical ones, across which as well "assertion and denial, celebration and complaint, authority and resistance" continuously shift figure and ground, Gestalt and paradigm, appealing to undecidables and aporias, as when Geertz muses about the place of Islam in Indonesia, noting that in his several decades of observation its role has dramatically shifted several times—itself a sociological and historical comparativist observation. His recent essay on Gus Dur Wahid shows that he remains a shrewd and incisive commentator on Indonesia. But about Islam's place he rather wishes to leave himself open to being "of many minds."

PART THREE: ON THE TRAIL OF AN ANTHROPOLOGY TO COME

By way of conclusion, I would return our gaze to the three challenges of 1990s anthropology as sites of deep play, each providing its own slide show: (1) the reconstruction of society in the wake of obliviously caused social trauma and structural violence—call this, title the slide, the move from cockfight to buzkashi; (2) the changes in science institutions from the 1960s to the 1990s—call this, title this slide, the move from Union Carbide in Bhopal (and Institute, West Virginia) to the demands of ACT UP and patient groups for accountability in the technologies of what is made to live and who is let die; and (3) the immersion in the telemedia—call this, title this slide, "War Again, 9/11, Qandahar, and the Autoimmune Cultural Toxicities of CNN and al-Jazeera."

1. From Cockfight to Buzkashi

On September 31, 2001, General Amin Said Tariq of the Northern Alliance in Afghanistan was quoted in a *Boston Globe* headline: "It is time for the Americans to join the game," the Great Game of and for Central Asia, the game of buzkashi. American special forces were photographed astride Afghan steeds playing the game. Quite apart from one's political stand on just wars or effectiveness of global interventions, one wonders how we will play the buzkashi game with smart bombs, psycho-pharmacological uppers for long range flights, nanotechnologies for smart protective uniforms, smart mobile surgical rooms, and whether we have, and how good are our game plans to pick up the land mines, destroyed schools, water systems, battered bodies and minds. Like the cockfight for an earlier era of violence, this buzkashi focuses our attention today again on violence, bare life, and states of exception. Buzkashi becomes an icon for the shift from disciplinary societies to societies of control (those that depend less on territorial integrity than on statistics, flows, codes, networks, and standards, and which when attacked create new zones of indistinction).

2. *From Union Carbide in Bhopal to the Demands of ACT UP and Patient Groups for Accountability*

The biopolitics of globalization are again at center stage, and at the center of these new ethical and political vortices are battles over the technosciences and biotechnologies themselves.

Cliff challenged us a few years ago to extend interpretivist approaches to the forms of life associated with "loose assemblages of differently focused, rather self-involved, and variably overlapping research communities in both the human and the natural sciences." He wrote: "Of all the sorts of work that go on under the general rubric of the human sciences, those that devote themselves to clarifying the forms of life lived out . . . in connection with linear accelerators, neuroendocrinological labs, the demonstration rooms of the Royal Society, astronomical observations, marine biology field stations, or the planning committees of NASA, are the least likely to conceive their task as limited to making out the intersubjective worlds of persons. Machines, objects, tools, artifacts, instruments are too close at hand to be taken as external to what is going on; so much apparatus, free of meaning. These mere 'things' have to be incorporated into the story, and when they are the story takes on a heteroclite form—human agents and nonhuman ones bound together in interpretivist narratives." After cautiously acknowledging the "ill-formed and variable, uncertain opening probes in an . . . ill-marked enquiry"— but I would say rapidly burgeoning field of science studies, (the anthropologies of Bruno Latour and Donna Haraway, Emily Martin, Rayna Rapp, Deborah Heath, and Karen-Sue Taussig, Steve Shapin and Simon Shafer, Sharon Traweek and Joe Dumit, Paul Rabinow and Lawrence Cohen, Kim and Mike Fortun, Adryana Petryna and Joao Biehl, Byron and Mary-Jo Good, Chris Kelty and Hannah Landecker, Jennifer Mnookin, Heinrich Schwarz, Kaushik Sunder Rajan, Cory Hayden, Margaret Lock, Gary Downey, and many others, myself included)—he notes, "Sciences, physical, biological, human, or whatever, change not only in their content or their social impact (though they do, of course, do that . . .) but in their character as a form of life, a way of being in the world" (AF).

What I want to mark here is a set of double movements that Cliff

marked ahead on the trails of an anthropology to come, the double movement between lives and works, the coming inevitably onto the scene after
the fact, *after the fact* in search of and *after the fact* belated, the world-
historical narratives, such as they are (bracketed as Lyotard would say, or
ironized with Geertzian caution), nonetheless world-historical narratives
(political master stories of modernization, or of anti-colonialism, "those
were the Bandung days," "the days of May 1968") bursting from time
to time into local worlds, and at other times carrying those local worlds
along with the spinning of the globe and the spinning of webs of significance and meaning, cosmic, scientific, metaphysical, and moral-ethical.

These doublings, hauntings, and phantasmagoria, tools of poesis,
praxis, and gesture, mark out an anthropology to come, a justice to come,
a community to come.

But the cockfights of science already are registered in rich accounts
by scientists themselves and by observers of their forms of life: François
Jacob's much admired autobiography, much cited by scientists, provides
an exemplary account of two trained roosters beak to beak in, as well, a
metaphysical and cosmic competition with God:

> Seminars, true rites of initiation, free-for-alls. . . . That day an American
> biochemist . . . The audience interrupted incessantly. . . . Chopping up his
> discourse with questions . . . badgering him, provoking him, nipping at his
> heels like excited puppies. . . . As for [Sol] Spiegelman, he was not easily
> confounded . . . he listened to comments and criticisms while playing with
> a piece of chalk in the fashion of a Hollywood gangster with a coin. . . .
> The deathblow came later in a cafe on the Boulevard Pasteur . . . the theory
> was dissected, torn apart, shredded into tiny pieces. Bit by bit, the bull
> weakened. A final thrust of [Jacques] Monod's descabello. The bull's final
> spasm. And resistance ceased. All this amidst laughter and joking. . . . *Two
> trained roosters beak to beak* vying with humor and sarcasm. . . . a will to
> power . . . a desire for intellectual domination . . . a world full of gaiety, of
> the unexpected, of curiosity, of imagination. A life animated as much by
> passion as by logic. Science meant for me the most elevating form of revolt
> against the incoherence of the universe. Man's most powerful means of
> competing with God; of tirelessly rebuilding the world while taking account
> of reality. (Jacob 1988, 215)

There is a richness, a *jouisance,* a gamble with passion, in the sport of
science, and also metaphysical depth, an agon with the mysteries of the
universe and life, not just an aesthetic harmony or a pleasure in technical

skill. As the Polish-born physicist, from the spa town and Hassidic seat of Rymanov in Galicia, I. I. Rabi puts it:

> Some of the young people I see, who are very good, take physics . . . as a system you can do things with, can calculate something with, and they miss . . . the mystery of it: how very different it is from what you can see, and how profound nature is. . . . There is no good translation of a *Witz*. It's a joke or a trick. It's the use of this kind of witty trick that I have always liked about physics. . . . I have always taken physics personally. . . . It's between me and nature. (Rabi 1960)

This metaphysical depth is often folded—like a double helix—against cultural traditions, historical experiences, and community structures. Some of the productive tensions and synergistic reinterpretations between scientific rationalities (such as they are in a post–Ludwig Fleck, Tom Kuhn, Bruno Latour, and Peter Galison era) and Christian and Jewish traditions have been explored, but one wonders in today's world why more has not been done with Hindu, Buddhist, Confucian, and Islamic traditions that lie in the background of some of the world's greatest scientists: Homi Bhabha, Vikram Sarabai, Ramanujan, Chandrasekar, Abdus Salam, Ghovind Khoranna, and now the Brahmin and Muslim creators of "the Hindu bomb"—Raj Ramana the classical pianist and explorer of resonances between Buddhist logic and high energy physics, and Avul Pakir Jainulabdeen Abdul Kalam, the current President of the Republic of India who justifies with good cockfight and game theory logic, "strength respects strength."

Above all, the search for accountability has transformed the ways in which the institutions of science and the technosciences operate. Call it the transformation from big science and the national security state to science accountable to multiple constituents lest the complexity of the infrastructure become brittle and break down. The ethics of science— and the representations of science in both the epistemological (accuracy, reference, completeness) and political or stakeholders' senses—are no longer marginal issues left up to the sensibility of the researcher or expert. Across the sciences these are becoming matters for institutional review, efforts at transparency, and negotiations between publics and researchers over the propriety of research that involves people and publics. As the world becomes more integrated and interactive, questions of how information is collected, packaged, and made available as part of social institutions of reflexive or second-order modernization (to use Ulrich

Beck's terms) become more important and open to insistent questioning, and that detouring through media circuits of advertising, advocacy, and persuasion only make all the more suspect and subject to insistent questioning. Does a local population always have to benefit, or is there a place for presumed consent to collection of various sorts of human biology data (blood, feces, cheek swabs, genetic, epidemiological, pathology samples, medical records), which only after considerable processing can be turned into statistical and "evidence based" knowledge and pharmacological and medical products? The answers to these questions are not in, but they are today central questions publicly debated and politically negotiated—from Iceland's experiment to allow deCode Corporation to link data banks of medical records, genealogies, and DNA samples, to the Harvard–Millennium Pharmaceuticals project in China to collect DNA samples from populations in Anhui Province—and are not easily swept under the carpet. The biosciences are a deep play that directly pose questions of who shall live and who shall die, and that exert pressure toward new institutions of reflexive modernization or deliberative democracy in some of the most difficult areas of human experimental trials, informed consent, privacy and surveillance, patents and ownership of biological information, and the power of huge amounts of investments of not just money and power but also ideology and fantasy.

3. *"War Again, 9/11,* Qandahar," *and the Autoimmune Cultural Toxicities of CNN and al-Jazeera*

No consideration of the current condition can avoid the new fabric of interacting media which have changed the calculus of, and conditions of possibility for, governance and legitimacy, of what democracy could possibly mean, of who speaks for whom, where all must play through the media, scientists and physicians as much as anyone, with anthropologists—for better and worse—far behind (running after the fact), and where the very use of telemedia has the effects, simultaneously, of both extending and undoing the messages, propaganda, persuasions, or pedagogies intended by the sender or patron, and where the truth is less hidden than partially revealed in measured and calculated unveilings that blur truth and falsity, that, as Hannah Arendt once said hide truth in the open where it can be assumed to be false, contaminated, or doctored, and is so by its very nature, without being any less the truth.

While Cliff has never devoted much attention to the telemedia, he has directed attention to the affective and cognitive, metaphorical and interpretive, tactics that form its basis. Symbolic anthropology and its morphing into interpretive anthropology can provide tools probing both cultural-philosophical meaning-making and also the sociology of cultural meanings and their operation as, and in, fields of power. For me, one of the tasks of anthropology is to do the anthropology—cultural and social analysis—of communities of social thought and social theory itself. It is not very interesting after a while to simply debunk efforts at pattern recognition, generalization, comparison, model building, formalizations-in-the-service-of-models against which complex realities can be approximated, good-enough theory for pragmatic needs, and the like, as if they were misunderstood as universal and eternal truths. It is the recognition of immanent cultural critique, the play of communities of social thought against one another (not, Cliff, "recriminations") that anthropology often is particularly well poised to place into the interpretive cockfight arena for us all to see the passions and irrationalities, as well as reasons and calculations, and social structures and cultural legitimations at play.

≈

I END HERE my marginalia, commentaries, misreadings, and *hashiyeh* in the hopes that they may serve as a small return gift to an extraordinary teacher and writer. Cliff, thank you!

NOTE

1. This remains a stylistically brilliant essay and homage to the "phenomenology" of Alfred Schutz, a genre—of which I am fond—of testing European theories with non-European materials, ideally in the end also retooling the theories. Gananath Obeyesekere's *Medusa's Hair* is another such brilliant example. But as ethnography, it raises, as the cliché goes, maybe not more questions than it answers, but many unanswered questions. This is particularly so in the aftermath of 1965. My own imagination for Bali is still profoundly marked by my, much later, visit to Bali with Byron and Mary-Jo Good, and meeting one of our colleagues whose passport continues to be marked as belonging to a "communist" family, and who thereby is prevented from holding any public position, including teaching in the university. He was a child in 1965 and lost both parents. The position of living amongst those one knows or suspects of killing one's parents, perhaps, only intensifies the tension surrounding the public masques and forms of address, time, and other social markers, that Cliff raises in this essay, and more flexibility in "Deep Play." It certainly puts a different spin on the implications, long "After the Fact." In a recent series of public discussions with refugees from social upheavals, preceding each performance of Peter Sellars's production of Euripedes' "The Children of Herakles" at the American Repertory Theatre, I heard an almost identical observation from a young Bosnian woman, now studying at Boston University, speaking of living together with the killers of one's relatives, "It is a small society, and everyone knows . . ." While severe mental illness involves very different sorts of dynamics, Byron Good's work in Indonesia on the episodic course of psychoses, in their cultural expressions and social responses among families, also adds layers of questions to the general

account of cultural psychology in Java (and Bali). I note these subsequent ethnographic benchmarks not as *criticism* of Cliff's work, but as an ongoing form of ethnographic *critique* that *builds upon,* and is able increasingly to incorporate more kinds of ethnographic, historical, cultural, and psychological materials. The provocations (to universal psychologies) and questions (for ethnographic method) raised by "Person, Time, and Conduct," are such that the essay, I think, can no longer be used in the classroom by itself as a self-contained essay, but requires additional materials to think with. That is, as they say these days, a feature, not necessarily, a bug.

REFERENCES

Geertz, Clifford. 1995. *After the Fact: Two Countries, Four Decades, One Anthropologist.* Cambridge: Harvard University Press.
Jacob, François. 1988. *The Statue Within: An Autobiography.* New York: Basic Books.
Rabi, I. I. 1960. *My Life and Times as a Physicist.* Claremont, CA: Claremont College.

Speaking to Large Issues
The World, If It Is Not in Pieces

A BRIEF QUOTE FROM Clifford Geertz reflecting on field work, in *After the Fact,* will begin to identify my concerns. In sum, he says,

> It is a matter of living out your existence in two stories at once. . . . One of these stories is the familiar one of the anthropologist projecting him- or herself onto the local scene as a minor actor, odd but harmless, and a solemn observer, searching out assorted facts. The other is the less familiar one, rarely recounted, of his or her attempt to maintain such a reduced and specialized persona amid the currents and cross-currents of world-scale politics. . . . You may set out to isolate yourself from cosmopolitan concerns and contain your interests within hermetical contexts. But the concerns follow you. The contexts explode. (Geertz 1995, 94–95)

Mostly, in his ethnographic work, Geertz himself has told one of these stories, that of the local scene.[1] Yet the double life of the fieldworker shows up more in his essays, and in his recent variations in autobiography; as for example in commenting on the moral dilemma of sharing or not sharing one's typewriter with a local informant of modest resources who dreams of becoming a writer; and on being sought out, in the late 1950s, by a group of earnest Balinese who wanted to have it confirmed by an American that the Soviet Union had indeed put a moon up in the sky. For if even an American would admit it, it must be true.

That concern with "the larger picture," with the world beyond the village, is I think continuously present in Geertz's work. For one thing, I see it in his insistence that in anthropology small facts can speak to large issues, when many of his colleagues in the discipline, after all, have seemed content to let their small facts speak to issues that are likewise rather small.[2] In some periods, the concern may not have been so noticeable, yet still contrapuntally present in his writings. At other times, it turns into more of a preoccupation. "The next necessary thing," he proposes toward the end of *Works and Lives* (1988, 47), is "to enlarge the possibility of intelligible discourse between people quite different from one another in interest, outlook, wealth, and power, and yet contained in a world where, tumbled as they are into endless connection, it is increasingly difficult to get out of each other's way." And along related lines, in the final chapter of *Available Light,* his most recent book, he portrays the world at the end of the twentieth century; he notes that "a much more pluralistic pattern of relationships among the world's peoples seems to be emerging," but that "its form remains vague and irregular, scrappy, ominously indeterminate"; and he suggests that what political theory should now do is to participate in the construction of "a practical politics of cultural conciliation" (2000, 256).

This is very recent Geertz. But I believe that the interest in large issues, the sense of coexistence of local and cosmopolitan stories, really goes back a half century or so, to the formative experiences of fieldwork in the period we may now describe as "early postcolonial." It was an era of excitement, and not least some optimism, where those new nations had "charismatic leaders," like Nehru, Nasser, Nkrumah, and of course Soekarno, and not yet, or at least not yet recognizedly, the despotisms and kleptocracies associated with a later period. Being a witness to Indonesian life in that period, I believe, could both shape a perspective and define a horizon. Again, President Soekarno was one of those charismatic heroes of an independence struggle, and the emergence in world politics of what would become the Third World had its perhaps most renowned symbolic site in the Indonesian city of Bandung. These were, as Geertz has later put it, "the Bandung days."

But academic settings count as well. It was likewise a time when scholars were busily remapping the world, and Clifford Geertz had his significant share of such activity, not least with the Committee for the Comparative Study of New Nations at the University of Chicago. Perhaps I should insert that among the commentators here, I am no doubt unusual in that my personal interactions with Clifford Geertz have been limited; I claim largely a view from afar, although from that vantage point my attention to his evolving thought and writing has been fairly constant. In any case, I believe I first came across Geertz's work, probably also unusually, in the volume *Old Societies and New States* (1963), a collaborative effort of that Committee. The book, which he edited and for which he also wrote a chapter, may not by now seem very central to Geertz's long-term contributions to anthropology, and it is distinctly a document of its era. Nonetheless, he draws attention to the connection between that book, and generally his time with the Committee for the Comparative Study of New Nations, and his current concerns, as he dedicates the concluding chapter of *Available Light* to the memory of the sociologist Edward Shils, a founding father of the Committee.

What Geertz took on, in his contribution to *Old Societies and New States,* was "The Integrative Revolution: Primordial Sentiments and Civil Politics in the New States." It is a wide-ranging essay, drawing on brief interpretations of the state of affairs in seven countries of South and Southeast Asia, the Middle East and Africa, and through the somewhat uncertain workings of oral and sometimes written tradition of a discipline such as anthropology, it may now be referred to most often as a source of a concept of "primordialism." We could note here, first, that the concept came from Edward Shils (1957); and second, that Geertz's actual understanding of primordialism seems rather different from what it may occasionally have been taken to be. Those primordial attachments stemming from the "givens" of blood, speech, custom, and so on, noted Geertz (1963, 109) immediately, are *assumed* givens, "as culture is inevitably involved in such matters"; which means, in a latter-day vocabulary, that primordialism is indeed socially constructed. Yet when people define things as real, they are real in their consequences; and these attachments indeed keep on having consequences.

In his early essay Geertz thus dwelt on the strains between divisive primordial sentiments and the push toward an overarching political regime in many new states; the strain between identity and recognition on the one hand and progress, efficiency and justice on the other. Again, the time of writing was one when the inclination was to take a fairly optimistic view of the future of the newly independent countries, and Geertz's argument was generally that through compromises between primordial attachments and civil politics, compromises that varied from one place to the other, the countries he discussed seemed to muddle through. In the following years, some of them did less than that—Sri Lanka, Lebanon, Nigeria— and such failures surely had their part in the decline of optimism. Yet it appears to me that as he returns to similar issues in *Available Light,* in arguing for that "practical politics of cultural conciliation," Geertz has maintained a consistent position.

So let us quickly come back to the present. In *Available Light,* in the final chapter titled "The World in Pieces: Culture and Politics at the End of the Century," but not only there, and also more occasionally, before that, both in *Works and Lives* and in *After the Fact,* I find Geertz increasingly turning explicitly to some large issues—of increasing global interconnectedness generally, or the upheavals of the world after the Cold War particularly.

Anthropologists have characteristically been merchants in astonishment, he already told us once (Geertz 1984, 275), and in a time of global flux, we use astonishing juxtappositions as one way of sensitizing our listeners and readers and ourselves to what is going on and what now goes together. In *Available Light* (2000, 247) Geertz has British bankers in Singapore gambling on Kobe earthquakes and Saudi production targets, in *Works and Lives* (1988, 133), Tongan running backs with the Washington Redskins.

Indeed the end of the twentieth century, and the beginning of a new millennium, finds humanity facing some new circumstances, and that necessarily affects the human sciences as well. Again, scholars are redrawing their map the world. Geertz argues that the cultural organization of the modern world ought now to be anthropology's proper subject, but that its old "cookie-cutter concept of culture" is no longer workable in the world of infinite connection (2000, 248). We must think again, for one thing, about how—or how not—to write anthropology: "Ethnographers have now to do with realities with which neither encyclopedism nor monographism, world surveys nor tribal studies, can practically cope. Something new having emerged both in 'the field' and in 'the academy,' something new must appear on the page" (1988, 148).

But what, then, can anthropology do? It seems reasonable to bring up the question of small facts and large issues again. In that period of now a little more than a decade that scholars, and some perhaps not quite so scholarly competitors, have once more been remapping the global landscape, some have been marketing what are purportedly very big facts—what one prominent participant in the trade, *New York Times* columnist Thomas Friedman, has identified as the genre of "The One Big Thing" (1999, xviii). Some of these grand narratives may already be fading away—"the end of history"—others are still with us: "the clash of civilizations," perhaps "the coming anarchy," certainly Friedman's own global marketplace with its stampeding "electronic herd" of investors.[3] (Those British bankers in Singapore are presumably somewhere in that herd.) If these stories do not necessarily homogenize the world, they do portray it as some kind of whole, rather than disconnecting its parts.

Again, what can anthropology do now? Can we do anything effectively to contribute to a public intellectual exchange over where the world is today, and where it might be heading? Or more precisely, in the context of this session, what does one particular anthropologist do to speak to large issues? In *Available Light*, Geertz (2000, 221ff.) states and exemplifies his position. Responding to "One Big Thing" stories—he specifically identifies Samuel Huntington's "clash of civilizations" scenario—anthropologists can hardly just go on offering another infinity of ethnographic facts. Still, he asserts that he is "an ethnographer, and a writer about ethnography, from beginning to end," and notes, moreover, that "I don't do systems." The latter, of course, might seem like a surprising claim from someone who has earned a part of his reputation from a series of essays analyzing religion, and ideology, and common sense, and art, as "cultural systems." But perhaps that is a matter of the past, and in any case, this is hardly the kind of systems he has in mind.

My own preferences may be a little different here. The gap between American and European anthropologies may no longer be what it has been, and they may no longer be easily told apart, even if there continue to be those in my part of the world who are less than enthusiastic about subversive influences from this side of the Atlantic. Nonetheless, whether we talk about this in terms of "systems" or not, it may be a European streak in my anthropology, perhaps related especially to an old fondness for what I believe Clifford Geertz has somewhere called "cloth-cap anthropology," which would lead me to favor some more robust sociological framing in the quest to understand precisely that cultural organization of the contemporary world.[4]

Yet let us leave that aside. What Geertz does identify as a resource of anthropology in understanding the global present is the particular kind of cosmopolitanism that he finds in "its determination to look beyond the familiar, the received and the near at hand"—"the considering together of what normally is not considered considerable together" (2000, 251). Comparison, that is to say, continues to be a major ingredient of Geertzian anthropology, from *Old Societies and New States* all the way to *Available Light*. But the style of comparison, as Renato Rosaldo (1999, 32–33) has pointed out in another collective effort to celebrate as well as scrutinize Clifford Geertz's work, is of a special kind, taking central concepts and exploring their connections and range of meanings through varied human contexts; inspired, it seems, by a Wittgensteinian sense of family resemblances.

One comment on this would be that a renewed, and rethought, use of comparison may well be one way of converting our ethnographic small facts into an asset in speaking to large issues—there are other indications of this (see, by way of comparison, Gingrich and Fox 2002). Rather than "One Big Thing" stories, we may favor identifying recurrent themes with their variations. There may be more ways of doing this, and in any case we would hardly all be able to do it in the particular way that Geertz goes about it. In most cases, probably, it would entail dealing with the ethnographic inventory of the discipline rather more as a shared resource, and cultivating skills of synthesis.[5]

But I would like, in conclusion, to point to another issue in the kind of understanding of the world that Geertz seems now to be working out. In his essay in *Old Societies and New States,* he made a plea for a better understanding of primordial attachments. In *Available Light,* in that final chapter, this is again the focus. The world scene, he notes, is "growing both more global and more divided, more thoroughly interconnected and more intricately partitioned, at the same time. As the one increases, so does the other" (2000, 246). And so on one side of this equation, there is "the world in pieces." As he also argues, "in a splintered world, we must address the splinters" (221). The identities continuously exemplified are those which in *Old Societies and New States* would have been identified as primordial: ethnic, national, linguistic, religious. And Geertz observes that there is indeed a continuity between the major changes of the 1950s and the 1960s and those of the 1990s, for in both periods what forms the background of a reaffirmation of such identities is the fall of empires. And in both periods it turns out that the relationship between splinters and whole is a different one from that of the old Western European notion of the nation-state.

All the same, I wonder about the other side of the equation, that of the world growing more global, more thoroughly interconnected. Cosmopolitanism may be a keyword here; it seems now to show up with increasing frequency in Geertzian texts, although possibly not always with the same thrust.

As Rosaldo continues his analysis of Geertz's mode of comparison, he notes that while Geertz takes barriers erected by cultural differences seriously, he also has a vision of ethnography as a tool by which people can come to understand the differences, and establish a vocabulary for speaking to one another. I think that herein lies a significant part of the cosmopolitanism of anthropology; a sense of the world as a whole, but combined with a respect for, or even appreciation of, diversity. And I do indeed think of Clifford Geertz as a cosmopolitan—more precisely what Kwame Anthony Appiah (1996) among others have recently described as a "rooted cosmopolitan," strongly connected to one place in the world and yet engaging with other ways of being human.

The rootedness is there, I would suggest, a little parenthetically, in a special although multifaceted relationship between his writings and American thought, in the way Geertz has continuously sought intellectual stimulation from American sources (not that others are missing), ranging from John Dewey by way of Kenneth Burke to Jerome Bruner; not necessarily everyday references among anthropologists. I believe it is also noticeable in the way that in *Works and Lives* (1988), he can incisively analyze the writings of Malinowski, Evans-Pritchard, and Lévi-Strauss, but eventually seems to have a more tender understanding of Ruth Benedict, and her attempt, by way of portraying the strange Japanese, to tell her compatriots about themselves. And I detect this rootedness, too, in his personal style of writing, with its precise deployment of American colloquialisms and occasional but no doubt stylistically very deliberate appeal to what seems like a culturally specific vocabulary of common sense. This rootedness, this cultural thickness as it were, is something that for me adds significantly to the pleasure of reading Geertz.

Yet as far as cosmopolitanism is concerned, that inclination toward looking beyond the familiar and the received, toward considering things together that have otherwise been kept apart, that openness to "another country heard from," can hardly now belong to anthropologists alone. If the world is not only in pieces, not only splintered, we should perhaps not think of addressing the splinters as our single task. We certainly cannot fail to notice the splintering, the spectacular clashes linked to primordialism on the global scene—as newsmedia editing strategy has it, "when it bleeds it leads." Yet from the times when primordial sentiments were contrasted with the civil politics of new states, to the present when they are set against global connectedness, the scholars mapping changes in the world may have been a bit inclined toward underestimating the cultural complexity of what is occurring on the other side of the equation, where a variety of people may also be motivated by their personal experiences of interconnectedness to identify with humanity in its diversity.[6]

Perhaps the identities growing here are sometimes not so culturally thin. Perhaps we can sometimes even witness that there is, in a sense, a kind of primordialization of cosmopolitanism going on, although often less spectacular. This will also have its implications for the way we do ethnography. Those contexts referred to in my beginning quote will explode again and again. But as the world is at the beginning of this century, we should hope that there is something other than pieces to look for. And as the final few words in *Available Light* instruct us, there is yet "the moral obligation to hope."

NOTES

1. Given what I take to be a reluctance on Geertz's part to appear very noticeably in person in his ethnography—with the famous exception of the opening scene in the essay on the

Balinese cockfight—I can see why the double existence of the fieldworker does not feature so prominently in it. For to the extent that there is really some tendency for the stories to be separate, the fieldworker may be the main connecting link, and their combination might inevitably turn into what he might see as the wrong kind of person-centered ethnography.

2. I realize that I interpret "large issues" in a somewhat narrow sense here, as a matter of social scale. Issues can be large in other ways as well.

3. The "One Big Thing" stories referred to here, of course, apart from Friedman's, are those of Fukuyama (1992), Huntington (1996), and Kaplan (e.g., 2000).

4. Geertz has commented rather ironically on this gap, as it was at an early 1960s Cambridge conference, in *After the Fact* (1995, 116–17). Yet certainly there would be American commentators as well, some of them close to Geertz, who would also be inclined to put more sociology into cultural analysis; see for example, Ortner (1999) and Sewell (1999). As far as American, and specifically Geertzian, transatlantic influence is concerned, let me also just note that what was presumably the first "HyperGeertz" comprehensive, contextual, and referential bibliography and mediagraphy was on an Austrian website (www.iwp.uni-linz.ac.at/lxe/sektktf/GG/HyperGeertz.html).

5. For some more discussion of this, and of the relationship of anthropologists to the genre of macro-scenarios generally, see Hannerz (2003).

6. For a comment on this in relation to *Old Societies and New States,* see Spencer (1997, 7).

REFERENCES

Appiah, Kwame Anthony. 1996. Cosmopolitan Patriots. In Martha C. Nussbaum et al., *For Love of Country,* ed. Joshua Cohen. Boston: Beacon Press.

Friedman, Thomas. 1999. *The Lexus and the Olive Tree.* London: HarperCollins.

Fukuyama, Francis. 1992. *The End of History and the Last Man.* New York: Free Press.

Geertz, Clifford. 1963. The Integrative Revolution: Primordial Sentiments and Civil Politics in the New States. In *Old Societies and New States,* ed. Clifford Geertz. New York: Free Press.

———. 1973. *The Interpretation of Cultures.* New York: Basic Books.

———. 1984. Distinguished Lecture: Anti Anti-Relativism. *American Anthropologist* 86: 263–78.

———. 1988. *Works and Lives.* Stanford: Stanford University Press.

———. 1995. *After the Fact.* Cambridge: Harvard University Press.

———. 2000. *Available Light.* Princeton: Princeton University Press.

Gingrich, Andre, and Richard G. Fox, eds. 2002. *Anthropology, by Comparison.* London: Routledge.

Hannerz, Ulf. 2003. Macro-Scenarios: Anthropology and the Debate over Contemporary and Future Worlds. *Social Anthropology* 11: 169–87.

Huntington, Samuel P. 1996. *The Clash of Civilizations and the Remaking of World Order.* New York: Simon and Schuster.

Kaplan, Robert D. 2000. *The Coming Anarchy.* New York: Random House.

Ortner, Sherry B. 1999. Introduction. In *The Fate of "Culture,"* ed. Sherry B. Ortner. Berkeley: University of California Press.

Rosaldo, Renato I., Jr. 1999. A Note on Geertz as a Cultural Essayist. In *The Fate of "Culture,"* ed. Sherry B. Ortner. Berkeley: University of California Press.

Sewell, William H., Jr. 1999. Geertz, Cultural Systems, and History: From Synchrony to Transformation. In *The Fate of "Culture,"* ed. Sherry B. Ortner. Berkeley: University of California Press.

Shils, Edward. 1957. Primordial, Personal, Sacred and Civil Ties. *British Journal of Sociology* 8: 130–45.

Spencer, Jonathan. 1997. Post-Colonialism and the Political Imagination. *Journal of the Royal Anthropological Institute* 3: 1–19.

Byron Good and
Mary-Jo DelVecchio Good

On the "Subject" of Culture
Subjectivity and Cultural Phenomenology
in the Work of Clifford Geertz

W HEN RICK SHWEDER AND WE began talking about organizing this event—two years ago at a similar panel organized for
Jerome Bruner—we discussed asking the Society for Psychological Anthropology to sponsor the gathering, as they had the Bruner panel. In
Bruner's case, the reasons were quite obvious. "Cultural psychology" is
a key part of the Bruner corpus. In the case of Clifford Geertz, it is somewhat less obvious. For while he has turned his attention systematically
from one domain to the next—religion, ecology in *Agricultural Involution,* economic development in *Peddlers and Princes,* Balinese kinship, the
social history and stratification of an Indonesian town, and the state and
polity of Negara—in each case demonstrating that cultural patterns are
constitutive, essential, not accidental to their understanding, Geertz has
never taken on psychology in the same fashion. Several of his essays—
notably "Person, Time, and Conduct in Bali," and "From the Native's
Point of View"—examine "the problem of the self—its nature, function,
and mode of operation" in Bali, Java, and Morocco. But none constitutes
a full blown cultural psychology. Despite this, we will argue that Geertz
has elaborated a view of subjectivity and the relation of the subject to
culture, which, while seldom noted, lies at the heart of the entire corpus,
whatever specific he is addressing. It is our goal here to review the lineage
of these ideas in light of current debates about subjectivity, in which diverse poststructuralist and linguistic theories vie with psychological and
phenomenological accounts, and to raise questions about where Geertz's
ideas might take us in the future.

In 1969, having completed a three-year degree in comparative religion
at Harvard Divinity School, I (BG) drove to Chicago to begin anthropology; Mary-Jo took a leave from the Social Relations Department at Harvard to join me for the year.[1] These were times both exciting and awful—
marked by the deaths of Martin Luther King and Robert Kennedy, the

police riots of the Democratic National Convention, the invasion of Cambodia, and the trial of the Chicago Seven. They were wonderful times to be a student, however, with the invention of interpretive anthropology in full swing; the interdisciplinary Committee for the Comparative Study of New Nations in its tenth year, headed by Tom Fallers; Vic and Edie Turner hosting Thursday night seminars in their home in Hyde Park; reading groups taking on Marx and critical theory at Terry Turner's apartment; and fortuitously, Clifford Geertz in the final year of a ten-year stint at the University of Chicago. Professor Geertz was, that year, extraordinarily available to students, gracious and accommodating. When forty students showed up for his Seminar on Theories of Culture, he simply divided the class in two and taught it twice, meeting four times each week instead of two. He taught a lecture course titled "Indonesia and Morocco—An Uncontrolled Comparison," which many attended avidly. And when that wasn't enough for a small group of us, he invited us to his home each week to discuss books we wished to read on the anthropology of religion.

If Professor Geertz was our teacher for only one year, the reading list for his Theories of Culture seminar—and his books, of course—were to be our teacher for years to come. It was a remarkable reading list—277 books and articles, divided among thirteen sessions—that gives a glimpse of the theoretical origins of Geertz's work, seldom in full view in his footnotes or bibliographies. The thirteen sessions had titles in parentheses, indicating a loose grouping of sources bearing on a topic: Patterns; Symbols; Values and Norms; World View; Art; Categories, Classification, etc.; Science; Structuralism; Ideology; Change; Semantics; Phenomenology; and Psychology. Readings for the eleventh session, grouped under the heading "Semantics," will give a flavor: Albert's " 'Rhetoric,' 'Logic,' and 'Poetics' in Burundi"; Arewa and Dundes, "Proverbs and the Ethnography of Speaking Folklore"; two essays by Bernstein, including "Some Social Determinants of Perception"; Brown and Gilman's "The Pronouns of Power and Solidarity"; Kenneth Burke's "The Philosophy of Literary Form," "Terministic Screens," and the entire *Rhetoric of Religion;* an essay by Burling; Ernst Cassirer's book *Language and Myth;* Geertz's own essay "Linguistic Etiquette"; Greenberg's book *Language Universals;* a Goodenough essay on componential analysis; Izutsu on "Principles of Semantic Analysis"; Jakobson's "Concluding Statement: Language and Poetics"; Katz's *The Philosophy of Language;* Mazrui on the "Sociopolitical Functions of English Literature in Africa"; Pike on "Emic and Etic Standpoints"; Vygotsky's "Thought and Word"; and Whorf on "The Relation of Habitual Thought and Behavior to Language"—that was for

Tuesday, with a similar list under the heading of "Phenomenology" on Thursday!

It will be no surprise that literary theorists figured large in the reading list—though this was eons before anyone imagined a "narrative turn" in the social sciences. Kenneth Burke, Northrop Frye, Walker Percy, and Auerbach's *Mimesis,* along with Susanne Langer, of course, joined Gombrich on *Art and Illusion* and historian of Chinese thought Joseph Levinson. However, several intellectual threads of what might be called "cultural phenomenology," less often recognized but representing a critical strand for understanding Geertz's theorization of subjectivity, figured large on the reading list. Merleau Ponty, Alfred Schutz, and behind these the neo-Kantian Ernst Cassirer provided the basis for developing an anthropological phenomenology, a phenomenology absent a transcendental subject. Geertz's set of essays, "Religion as a Cultural System," "Ideology as a Cultural System," "Common Sense as a Cultural System," and "Art as a Symbolic System," represent a Schutzian exercise in describing phenomenological "perspectives" (explicated in Schutz's essays on "multiple realities"[2]), but with local symbolic systems providing the content and substance of each perspective. This anthropological elaboration on Schutz is grounded in the work of Ernst Cassirer and his vision of "symbolic forms" as mediating between Kant's a priori categories of mind and the perceived world, actively constituting "image-worlds" (in Cassirer's terms) of language and myth, religion, art, history, and science. But all of this becomes an *ethnographic* theory of subjectivity when made local, placed in "a small, shabby inland county-seat sort of place" that was Pare in Central Java in the 1950s, or in Bali or Sefrou, described by Geertz with similar flair. And for these, the ethnographies on the reading list are more relevant: Hallowell, particularly "The Ojibwa Self and its Behavioral Environment"; Godfrey Lienhardt's *Divinity and Experience;* Stanner's *On Aboriginal Religion* and "The Dreaming." In these, as in Geertz's ethnographies, the subject embodies culture, lives in a distinctive phenomenal world—spirits here, mystical powers there, particular categories of kin in each—and has access to that world through a set of embodied practices—Javanese meditation, Balinese dance, or simply growing up in a Balinese household—practices and encounters with realities that "clothe those conceptions with such an aura of factuality" (and you know the rest). In these, culture shapes "the behavioral environment," in Hallowell's terms, as well as the "selves" who inhabit that environment; and the "moods and motivations" incorporated into these selves are not limited to the religious perspective, but carry over into the "everyday," "common sense" world, making Protestants into capitalists, and perhaps even Santri into capitalists as well. Only time will tell about that.

But it is Geertz's explicit work on the person, or the self, that has had such profound influence on psychological anthropology.

> In all three of the societies I have studied intensively [he writes in "From the Native's Point of View"[3]], Javanese, Balinese, and Moroccan, I have been concerned . . . with attempting to determine how the people who live there define themselves as persons, what goes into the idea they have (but, as I say, only half-realize they have) of what a self, Javanese, Balinese, or Moroccan style, is. And in each case, I have tried to get at this most intimate of notions *not* by imagining myself someone else, a rice peasant or a tribal sheikh, and then seeing what I thought, but by searching out and analyzing the symbolic forms—words, images, institutions, behaviors—in terms of which, in each place, people actually represented themselves to themselves and one another.

It is this notion of the self or person as symbolic "all the way down" that contributed to a movement to investigate "the person" or "self" across cultures. It also initiated an important line of research and reflections on Javanese cultural psychology, from Ward Keeler to Steve Ferzacca's recent book, that respond specifically to Geertz's writings on Java.[4] And it is on these writings on the Javanese self that we would like to focus our attention for our few remaining minutes.

Most of you will recall Professor Geertz's elaborations of two sets of contrasts—*batin* and *lair,* glossed as "inside" and "outside," and *alus* and *kasar,* "refined" and "coarse"—through which Javanese, he says, pursue their efforts to be human, debating "reason and passion, the nature of time, or the reliability of the senses" with an "absolutely astonishing intellectual vitality." The goal of being *alus,* refined, pure, subtle, smooth, is pursued through a set of religious disciplines aimed at quieting the inner self, "thinning out" or "smoothing" one's emotional life, and by enacting a form of etiquette through which persons shape their outer or behavioral life to appear "predictable, undisturbing, elegant, and . . . choreographed." In *The Religion of Java,* this complex of symbolic action is shown to be rooted in *prijaji* religious practices, those distinctive Javanese forms of Hindu-Buddhist and Sufi exercises rooted in what is still called—by our Javanese psychiatrist friends, for example—*Filsafat Hidup Jawa,* the Javanese philosophy of life. It is this vision of cultural psychology, and of Javanese cultural psychology in particular, that we would like to query with three clusters of questions and ethnographic anecdotes.

First, what is the status of this complex of ideas and ideals, this pattern of managing self and the emotions, in Java today? One anecdote. I taught a course on "Culture, Emotions and Psychopathology" for master's degree students in psychology in Gadjah Mada University in 1996, shortly after we arrived as Senior Fulbright lecturers. In a session on culture and depression, we broke into small groups to discuss experiences students had had with depression or people they knew who had suffered severe depressions. I was only beginning to study Indonesian language at that time, and ran a small group, all young women, in English. Some of the students knew each other well; others in our group had only recently met. The first young woman to speak launched immediately into a story of her separation from her husband, her resulting bouts of depression, and her difficulties in deciding whether it was best for the children to remain with her husband or to seek a divorce. Soon she was crying, and the other students were stroking her arms, themselves in tears, joining the conversation. A second young woman in the class soon picked up a more difficult story—about how her father, a famous psychology professor, had taken up with another woman, lived openly with that woman though remaining married to her mother, deeply shaming the mother and the family, and about how she herself had become depressed, and was now less and less seen as a promising young scholar, overtaken by her younger sister, also studying psychology, who, by the way, lived with their father. Few in the group knew this student very well, but they were soon holding and stroking her as well, engaged in a remarkable bit of intimate reflection on their inner lives.

I should probably not have been as surprised as I was, although this intimacy and open expression of emotion was remarkably different from the style of managing affect I had expected to find, based on my reading about the Javanese self. These were psychology students, speaking English not Javanese, and this was of course 1996 at the cosmopolitan heart of Jogjakarta, not the 1950s in Pare, not *prijaji*, women not men, a different time, a different place. But it does raise questions about the status in Java today of what Cliff and Hildred observed about Javanese psychology as graduate students in the 1950s. We know there are continuities. An ontology of inner power, strength, force, achieved through a variety of practices old and new—for example, *tenaga dalam,* "inner power" meditation groups among students today replace many of the mystical sects popular in the 1950s and 1960s—still is central to understanding selfhood for a vast majority of Javanese we know. But Java is now a very complex meeting place of diverse transnational images and cultural and religious forms. Our Javanese goddaughter watches Javanese dance on television and immediately assumes embodied postures of classical Javanese culture. This shifts when *dangdut* music comes on, with young Islamic women covered with *jilbab* swaying to a kind of global Islamic rock. And when she puts on our earphones and listens to CDs of Motown or blues, she immediately begins to enact yet another culture. She is fluent in each, embodying one after the other with remarkable grace.

The questions we ask in this context are asked daily by our Javanese friends. What is happening to Javanese culture? What contours of Javanese personhood will emerge in this setting? What exactly constitutes "Javanese" subjectivity as we enter the twenty-first century? Are the old cultural forms that once shaped how Javanese spoke of the self and managed their emotions still relevant for current generations, and to the extent they are not, what has replaced them? Exploring new forms of Javanese subjectivity, emerging under quite new conditions, is a line of inquiry that follows naturally from the Geertzian corpus.

The second set of questions has to do with the studies of individual lives in relation to the cultural norms through which self and person are imagined. What are the relations among these cultural ideals of selfhood, these "symbolic forms—words, images, institutions, and behaviors" to which Geertz refers, and the enormous diversity of *individual* lives and psyches? How are these symbolic coordinates and cultural practices appropriated and integrated into their lives by individuals? Ethnographic accounts of Susanne Brenner and Leslie Dwyer show,[5] for example, how Islamic revivalism and donning the *jilbab* have very different meanings for individual women, and the same is true for the meditation practices of those we know. Our research with persons suffering serious mental illness and their families is a constant reminder of how individual life histories, personal psychologies, and Javanese ideals of personhood interweave. But sustained analysis of individual lives is all too seldom present in ethnographic writing.

In *After the Fact*, Geertz quotes a retired Nationalist Party leader talking, in 1971, about the terrible killings of 1965. This man concluded: "There is still a good deal of bad feeling around on the part of friends and relatives of the victims. But anti-Communism is now so strong here they don't dare say anything; they just conceal it, like good Javanese. I myself am as anti-Communist as I always was. But the real hatred, the murdering and being murdered, was a matter between Muslim militants and Communist ones." This murdering and being murdered is a matter for inquiry in and of itself, challenging *any* cultural psychology. But so too are the trauma and memories that mark the lives of individuals who lived through those desperate days. As Indonesians attempt, uneasily, to revisit 1965, even as new violence is afoot and more threatens, the study of trauma in individual lives, of how Indonesian cultural forms such as those Geertz describes shape memory and the management of the pain it produces, is not only more possible than before, it is even more desperately needed.

But such research requires theories and ethnographic practices that link investigations of symbolic forms with the lives of individuals. Psychology has been out of vogue for much of American anthropology since the late, over-reaching years of culture and personality theorizing. Geertz singled out for elaboration one crucial thread in American anthropological writing on the subject and subjectivity—a phenomenological subject linked to Hallowell and Sapir (and more ambivalently to Benedict), but traceable to the "Romantic" subject of German theorizing (including that of Herder, Humboldt, and Hamann, by Charles Taylor's reckoning[6]). Ironically, elaboration of a *cultural* theory of the person and subjectivity may have contributed to resistance to investigations of individuals, reluctance to link common symbolic forms to enormously diverse psychological experiences of particular Javanese. But surely, at a moment when anthropology self-consciously rejects essentialized representations of "cultures" and struggles to write about groups that appear as "a tangle of differences and similarities only half sorted out," as Geertz writes,[7] studies of subjectivity through investigations of individual lives, investigations of how individuals appropriate elements from increasingly discordant cultural forms available through diverse media, become more critical if we are to make any sense of contemporary "Javanese" personhood or subjectivity. And for this, elaboration of new theoretical constructs and ethnographic practices, and a willingness to engage psychology in a way that threatens to "reciprocally disequilibrate" both anthropology and psychology,[8] will be needed to extend the lineage Geertz continues to elaborate.

Finally, the story of the Nationalist Party leader's description of how "good Javanese," whether Muslim militants or former Communists, concealed their feelings and memories about the killings of 1965 raises a third set of questions. What is the relationship of the politically "hidden" to our understanding of subjectivity and subjective experience? What happens when that which has been widely presumed as simple "common sense" is suddenly felt by many in the society to be hegemonic, when broad segments of society recognize how state apparatuses have used cherished formulations of self and family to naturalize their power, when what is actually felt about public ideologies is concealed, when "subjectivity" is placed in tension with "subjection"? How can a careful cultural phenomenology, such as that pioneered by Geertz, contribute to an understanding of the hegemonic, or, in turn, of those moments when state ideologies are felt to lose their hold, seen as symbolic forms behind which corrupt elites hide their real motives rather than a "map" for an imagined community? How do we theorize Javanese subjectivity in moments of widespread cynicism and despair such as that resulting from the obvious failures of political reform—*reformasi*—since the fall of Soeharto? Or even more difficult, whose voice do we privilege when *we* see hegemony where many (but not all) members of a society see everyday reality?

When I assigned my psychology students in 1997 in Jogjakarta to interview young parents about what was different between how their parents raised them and how they were attempting to raise their own children, discussions of the authority role of the father and the order and "discipline" he maintains for his children were ubiquitous. But this was at precisely the moment that the Soeharto regime had launched a *Gerakan Disiplin Nasional,* a national discipline movement. The language of the state drew upon powerful symbols and affects of Javanese families, and, combined with memories of the terrible chaos of 1965 and thirty years of state propaganda that linked disorder and Communism, the call for "order" and "discipline" were psychologically powerful. Nonetheless, the mid-1990s was a time of enormous and widely recognized state corruption, and for many Javanese, such New Order symbols had lost much of their power. With typical Indonesian word play, *disiplin* was transformed into *di-silip in,* to have "slipped in," indicating with a wink how one had to slip money into one's driver's license whenever stopped by the police, or into the myriad of documents passed to government officials. "Hidden transcripts" were beginning to be less hidden, though the language of order and harmony continued to mask a will to power. Theorizing subjectivity under conditions such as these, amidst the decline of the New Order, thus required not only an understanding of the power of cultural forms to disguise the regime's actions and naturalize its notions of "order" but also an analysis of the ability of many Indonesians to provide their own critical readings of elite discourses. It required attention to political subjectivity and the place of the imagination in the constitution of the state and its power.

For a moment after Soeharto was thrown from power in 1998, the loose ideology of reform, or *reformasi,* mapped a potent new reality.

Balinese could stop concealing their rage behind a docile image of the PDI bull, friends told Mary-Jo, and the bull was redrawn on the party banners and logos to represent its actual fierceness. Supporters of Megawati could actually wear Democratic Party tee shirts—red with the image of the bull in black—rather than Chicago Bulls jerseys with Michael Jordan's name and numerals, which more covertly proclaimed their allegiance to "Ibu Mega" and their rejection of the New Order regime. But three years and three presidents later, the term *reformasi* now too is greeted with cynicism, and rogue elements of the state apparatus combine with parochial ethnic and religious leaders to loose new forms of violence in sites scattered about the archipelago. Cultural phenomenology needs to be extended to the complexities of political subjectivity under conditions such as these if we are to make anthropological sense of contemporary subjectivity in places like Indonesia.

We are at a moment in anthropology's history when no single theory of subjectivity will, or can possibly, suffice. Clifford Geertz has provided a remarkable synthesis of humanist theorizing of the subject. His work points naturally toward several complementary efforts, linked to psychoanalysis and studies of individuals, on the one hand, and to critical theory and studies of political subjectivity, on the other, which practitioners of interpretive anthropology are pursuing today. And in his latest writing, he continues to try to make sense of the dramatic changes transforming postcolonial societies such as Indonesia and Morocco over the past forty years, to explore the rise of new forms of both cosmopolitanism and parochialism, which constitute distinctive modernities that frame emerging subjectivities. Throughout this monumental work, Clifford Geertz has continued to reflect with great passion and insight on what it means to be human in very diverse—but always specific—times and places. For these profound contributions to anthropology and the human sciences, we join the participants in the symposium in paying him homage. And for his assuming that ancient and enduring role of teacher, we say simply, thank you, Cliff.

NOTES

1. Although written jointly by Byron and Mary-Jo DelVecchio Good, this paper was prepared to be read aloud by Byron Good. When the first person is used in the text, the "I" refers to Byron Good.

2. Alfred Schutz, *Collected Papers, vol. 1: The Problem of Social Reality* (The Hague: Martinus Nijhoff, 1971).

3. Quoted from Clifford Geertz, *Local Knowledge* (New York: Basic Books, 1983), 58.

4. Ward Keeler, *Javanese Shadow Plays, Javanese Selves* (Princeton: Princeton University Press, 1987); Steve Ferzacca, *Healing the Modern in a Central Javanese City* (Durham, NC: Carolina Academic Press, 2001).

5. Susanne Brenner, "Reconstructing Self and Society: Javanese Muslim Women and 'The Veil,'" *American Ethnologist* (1996): 673–97; Leslie Dwyer, "Making Modern Muslims: Embodied Politics and Piety in Urban Java, Indonesia" (PhD diss., Princeton University, 2001).

6. Charles Taylor, "Theories of Meaning," in his *Philosophical Papers, vol. 1: Human Agency and Language* (New York: Cambridge University Press, 1985), 248–92.

7. Clifford Geertz, *Available Light* (Princeton: Princeton University Press, 2000), 249.

8. Geertz, *Available Light,* 199.

Commentary

I HAVE NOT CHANGED my comments significantly from the form they took at the symposium at which I had a half-hour to respond. The number of papers necessitated that the reply to each be brief, and the variety of topics was such that I took an informal and unsystematic, rather ad hoc, approach to them. I am, as I made clear at the symposium, extremely indebted both to Richard Shweder and Byron Good for conceiving and organizing the event and to the various participants for giving their time and attention to my work and producing such perceptive and challenging discussions of it. The lightness of tone of my remarks conceals, as such lightness often does, the deep emotion I felt upon the occasion, and rereading the contributions, I feel now. It was a very personal occasion, despite the presence of many people. I trust that at least some of this will get through to the reader.

LAWRENCE ROSEN

The turn, starting most dramatically with the Vietnam period, toward a more open and direct expression of personal judgments in anthropology, has raised, as Lawrence Rosen, a half lawyer, half anthropologist hippogriff, is preadapted to recognize, some seriously complex issues for anyone claiming to be just giving the news please about other peoples' ways of going about things. The Olympian pose—that these things, strange as they may seem, are just out there and I only tell you that they are, whatever you do or don't think about the matter—is no longer a plausible stance, if it ever was. No one believes you anyway. Leaving the world alone is not something infra-lunary beings, as Paul Veyne would say, meaning us, can do. The recognition of the situated (and unreliable) nature of the observer, of the moral overtones of even the most thinned out, reductive, technically armored analysis, and of the fact that as humans are not Martians, treating them as though they were, strange objects in a featureless space, produces caricature . . . all these have brought, as

Larry points out, the old question back into our line of sight: "What is the right thing *for us* to do?" That is, what is the right thing to say, to write, to argue, to indict, to defend, and when need be, perhaps the most difficult thing of all, when ought we to hold our tongues. The human world is indeed various, puzzling, and impossible to sum up in simple good vs. bad formulae. But the matter can hardly be left at that.

This leaves us, as Larry says, with the question not *whether* to pass judgments, but *how*. How to phrase them, how to limit them, how to make them plausible, how not to fall in love with them. And, as he also says, my own approach here has been less head-on than oblique. The adjusted tone, the passing adjective, the parenthetical allusion, the glancing comment, the careful irony-thrown elbows and sideways kicks. The danger in this, of course, is the fact that judgments are being made, verdicts are being advanced, even sentences are being passed, may be missed altogether by the prosodically tone deaf. That has, indeed, sometimes been the case in my case: a quietness of comment being taken for an absence of it, a muffled view for no view at all. That's the danger, especially in these days of blare and polemic. But it seems to me a lesser danger than a loud and headlong parti pris moralism—stiff in opinions, as Dryden says, and always in the wrong. The judgin' business, as that famous Beyond the Fringe sketch has it, is a lark compared to goin' down the mines. And it is all too easy—to quote the late great jurist Paul Freund—to substitute the complacencies of voting for the strains of judging.

RICHARD SHWEDER

Richard Shweder's paper with its hard questions about relativism, pluralism, diversity, and the like takes us further into this whole wrenching issue. But, before trying to address the questions he poses as such, let me extend this notion that much of the "judgin'" that takes place in my work comes less in terms of explicit verdicts than through passing comments, insinuate phrases, over-the-shoulder, curve-ball tones of voice and the like, by taking issue with his recommendation that the best thing to do about my writing style is to "ignore it for the sake of getting on with a discussion of his ideas." (Jim Boon's piece is, of course, directed to this subject altogether, and I will deal with it . . . and with him . . . in a moment—or maybe a moment and a half.)

I do this not to defend my style (or styles) as such. Having toiled over it for so many years, I am quite aware of its deficiencies, and if I am not there is always a reviewer to remind me. The pleasures of the text are hard pleasures. I do it to question whether style and substance are so easily separable in such matters. Cyrano without his nose is, after all, not Cyrano, but just another hapless fop orating to a balcony. It is his style, and the pain that inhabits it, that makes him into a great romantic figure. I do not claim to be that, at least in public. But I do think that much of what I have to say inheres in how I say it, and that this is especially true when it comes to deciding about issues of judgment. To make up a Yogi Berra–ism: you can say a lot just by writing.

That aside, Rick's questions are indeed trenchant and very much to the point, so I will, of course, do my best to evade them. His wish to locate me vis-à-vis Richard Posner's utilitarian anti-moralism and Isaiah Berlin's Viconian humanism, between the lawyer-economist's certainty and the philosopher-historian's puzzlement, is an interesting notion, at least to me. Isaiah was, in fact, a personal friend (it was he who got me to Oxford for a year) from whom I learned an enormous lot, and whose voice, rapid, hectic, and all over the place, warm and engulfing, relentlessly comic, I can still hear fifteen years after, standing on a Manhattan street corner for a half hour with him, I last heard it. (Dizzy Gillespie was there too, but that's another story.) Posner, I have never met, and I can't say that his work—only a bit of which I have read, and most of that the fugitive stuff—has impressed me all that much.

Isaiah's great strength was his ability to get deeply enough into views foreign to his own, even antipathetic to them (for, a political actor and a bon vivant, he was anything but detached from the world, and I never knew him to be neutral about anything), to appreciate their force—something I don't see in Posner, who seems, often at least, to think he has things taped. Berlin is for that reason for me a much more shaking thinker: one who makes things harder, not easier. Posner is too ready with answers to suit me (though again, I can't claim detailed acquaintance with his work), and he seems to me more complacent about things than he, or anyone else, has at all earned the right to be. Isaiah's arguments are not fully adequate, as he himself insisted they could not be in the nature of the case. But they take us into the heart of the matter: how to decide and act when there are no answers in the back of the book. And that is my concern too, whatever differences I may have with him on this or that matter— for example, that forms of life are readily separable from one another and the natural focus of our moral concern. I don't think much of trying to judge whole societies, cultures, or historical periods—or schematized institutions, like infanticide, either: we can leave that to the ideologues.

All this doesn't go very far toward addressing the specific questions

Rick raises. But there is not world enough and time. He is right that I resist short abstract answers to broad theoretical questions. And I doubt there is more to *anything* that Montaigne imagined.

JAMES PEACOCK

With James Peacock's paper we turn more directly to "my place in the field," always a fascinating topic for an aging savant, who can discourse upon the subject for hours—to the relation of my work to our profession's self-conception, what it is it is supposed to be doing.

As he says, my aim has been to develop a way of studying systems of meaning, ways-of-being-in-the-world, forms-of-life, "culture" with as shuddering a set of quotes as I can devise, which would neither be a high church rationalism, which whatever the exotica it deals with, I regard structuralism as being, or a low church methodism, which is how I see "componential analysis." Whether this has had the salvationist effects Jim so generously says it has had, I don't rightly know—I'm too much focused on that damned horse and nail. But we don't seem to be in instant danger of running out of either flâneurs or barbarians. Which is probably just as well. As Cavafy almost says: such people are useful, what would we do without them?

But his point that both the impetus for my doing what I have been doing, developing and testing out ways of describing and conceptualizing "logico-meaningful" systems, and the resources for it as well, came in good part from outside, often from far outside, anthropology. Sapir and Benedict, as well as Kluckhohn and Redfield, were of course important, and so was E-P. But sociologists, Weber, Parsons, Goffman, or Schultz; psychologists, Bruner, Vygotsky; philosophers, Wittgenstein, Langer, Ryle, James; critics, Burke; poets, Stevens, Don Marquis, were at least as important. But even more critical was the fact that I came into anthropology from a background in the humanities and have never been fully deprogrammed, or even debriefed, never properly socialized. I have spent, by my count, no more than two and a half years in a purely anthropological setting in my half-century career, and much of that hiding from chairmen. . . . If, as the oldest living inhabitant, the wisdom-giver emerged blinking from his cave, I have any sage advice to give you young'ns out there, then, it is this: anthropology is too important to be left to anthropologists. Which, as he assigns books called THE GREAT WORK (I wish I had thought of that), I gather is Jim Peacock's view of things as well.

JAMES BOON

Then there is that other James: M. Boon, the man who made digression famous. Himself, perhaps the most distinctive stylist in anthropology, unless you count G. P. Murdock, he addresses himself, and addresses himself, and addresses himself to *my* style. "Shaggy sentences," "list-laden discursivity," "prosy maze," "wayward shuffle," "Geertzy *mots*" indeed! Quel chutzpah!

But seriously folks, the heart of Boon's message, here as just about everywhere else, is that solemnity and seriousness are not the same thing, and that those of us—he and I are alike in this, as in so much else, except for the ability to abide Frazer—unable to keep a wholly straight face when confronting the really important things of life have something of a problem when it comes to anthropological prose making. Comic gravity, a careless air in the face of hard reality is a difficult thing to bring off. You all know the line, dying is easy, comedy is hard. But I rather prefer a reworking of Dolly Parton's "it takes a lot of money to look this cheap"—viz.—"it takes a lot of sweat to sound this casual." Style is indeed a moral matter, but that is no excuse for dullness or staying too logical, and a "colloquial, caustic, scatter-shot" way of assembling evidence and passing judgments has much to be said for it, as does, to take Jim's case, never meeting a pun you don't like. This high occasion is, as I just mentioned, an opportunity for me to pass on tribal wisdom to the anthropological youth, whom I have never been able to convince that it pays, really pays in hard, tenurable cash and now and then a genuinely grateful business major, to be readable. Better over the top than under the pile.

But I pass the opportunity on to a more talented savage, Theodore Roethke, who knew what fate awaited the terminally "Academic":

The stethoscope tells what everyone fears
You're likely to go on living for years
With a nurse-maid waddle and a shop-girl simper
And the style of your prose growing limper and limper.

ULF HANNERZ

Ulf Hannerz, the only European anthropologist here, extends this general line of reflection on to the large scale of societies, of civilizations, of the world. As he notes, I have been concerned with "making small facts speak to large issues" from the very beginning, and for all my fascination, quite undimmed, with strange instances and odd detail (nothing is so interesting as something that doesn't fit), I have never seen anthropology as a boutique discipline peddling exotica to coffee-table consumers.

The question, of course, is how the devil to do this. How do you turn particular observations—a cockfight, a botched funeral, a sheep raid, market bargaining—into general comment—on violence, on faith, on imperialism, on social trust. And, as he also notes, one of the main areas in which I have tried to do this is with so-called primordial attachments. (Which, praise be to God, someone has finally gotten right: They are not natural givens or frozen history or the return of the repressed; they are cultural perceptions.) My first pass at this, in the New Nations book, is indeed more optimistic in tone than it would be were I to write it today, The "integrative revolution" I hoped for, the "modernization of primordial sentiments within the context of civil politics" has, like other expected revolutions, been rather postponed in many places and in some put off indefinitely. The roll call is horrifying: Rwanda-Burundi, Algeria, the Sudan, Kashmir, Sri Lanka, Eastern Indonesia, the southern Philippines, the Balkans, the Caucasus, Chiapas. One is anyway in no apparent danger in running out of hard cases: it all makes work, as Flanders and Swann used to say, for the working man to do.

In returning, a few passing essays over the years in between, to this subject in "The World in Pieces," I hoped to begin a deeper inquiry into these matters in a way that would make it all less promissory. I hope that piece—which was conceived and originally published separately from the other things in *Available Light*—concerned as it was with a critique of some master ideas of both political theory and anthropology (a *critique*, not a rejection), could be a more extended inquiry into a more immediate and more practical question: namely, whether a multiethnic democracy is possible, and whether we can see any movements, any possible paths, in that direction on the present scene.

If we think, for instance, of the three most formidable of the no longer so new, no longer so emerging states (or, as I would prefer, "countries"), Nigeria, India, and Indonesia, they are all vast assemblages of—well, of primordial attachments, barely reconciled. In the past, such polyglot, polycultural, polycredal entities have been contained, with more success or less, and for a time, in empires: the Ottoman, the Habsburg, the British, the Soviet. The nation state, as we know it in France, Italy, Brazil, Canada, the United States where it became the frame and foundation of popular government there, took several centuries to evolve from Westphalia, and it now seems, with the two world wars, to be creaking at the joints, dubiously transferable to such jagged places as Nigeria, India, and Indonesia.

The question of what form nonauthoritarian government might take, or might be struggling to take, in such places seems to me one that an anthropologist, trained to notice difference and see connection, is especially well placed to address. In any case, it is what I want to do if my strength holds out, and whether I get anywhere or not, it should be sociologically robust enough, and "cloth-cap" enough, to suit Hannerz, and cosmopolitan—rooted, primordial, or just plain determined—enough too.

MICHAEL FISCHER

One of the advantages of living a long time—at least I *think* it's an advantage—is that you get to see, in the work of younger colleagues, former students, and after-the-fact critics, something of what is to become of your work in the future—"what (as Foucault once said) your doing does." Now, when everything is coming up post, this can be a shaking experience. But it can also be, as with Michael Fischer's piece, a deeply reassuring one. Not only has not all been for naught (there is, after all, nothing so dead as a dead academic) but also one has started some fires that will burn in their own way, with their own fuel, to their own conclusions. If one wants one's work not to go out of date one should write (very, very good) poetry, not mess around in the human sciences, where the half-life of any idea or any reputation is may-fly in length. Who now reads Robert Lowie? Clark Wissler? Geoffrey Gorer?

Thus I am warmed, to keep the fire metaphor going, by the fact that one of the least tractable spirits in anthropology, someone who has gone his own way with flair and determination from the beginning, has found some things to bounce off against—turtles, metaphors, "comparative epistemology"—in my work. As Michael notes, much of what I have said has been derived, if often obliquely and with a twist, from others—Weber, Dilthey, Ricoeur, Ryle, Schutz, Kohut, the Parsons layer-cake, even, god save the mark, the old Panopticist himself, Bentham—so it is only proper that it be re-projected back into the wider stream of thoughts and thinkers exterior to, in some ways even orthogonal, to it.

Of these, perhaps the development that most interests me, and which I most regret not having done more with than the few odd pieces, general and project framing, I have produced, is "science studies." I never wrote the natural sequel to my "X as a cultural system" genre, "Science as a

Cultural System" (though I think *Available Light* is, to a degree, that), partly because I tired of the conceit (I didn't write "My Life as a Cultural System" either, though I threatened to), and partly because I realized that I didn't really believe in the "unity of the sciences" or that the destiny of anthropology was to become physics with the calculus removed. As Michael remarks, I did struggle to get the social study of science represented at the Institute, but was blocked by the natural science hard-liners who, for all their talk of the virtues of criticism, don't much like it when in comes from what they take to be the rabble. In any case, the project— "the study of science as a form of life"—thrives, both inside anthropology and just around it. I would, in my "revolt but don't be too revolting" sort of way, urge that we be sure to get somewhere rather far in understanding "science as we know it"—Fleck, Latour, Kuhn, and Galison—before wandering too far off into the distant realm of Muslim physics and Buddhist logic. But doubtless I will, as usual, and with good reason, not be listened to by those for whom the new always beckons and trespassing is a vocation. The future, as they say, lies ahead.

As for games, great and little, everything is becoming such right now (I write in the closing days of February, 2003, as the United Nations gathers to "finally" decide about the question of Iraq, and Afghanistan seems yesterday's war), and it is hard to know what to do with such imagery any more. Buzkashi and the cockfight are clearly the models of something, but what they are the models of (or, you should excuse the expression, "for") is still very much in the process of unfolding. One of the hard parts about being an anthropologist of Michael's sort and mine, those who chew at our pencils in worry over the moral implications of what we are writing, is that they are, those implications, usually concealed from us until it is rather too late to do anything very much about them. Whether the "biopolitics of globalization" will help with this problem or not (it sounds a bit grand to me), it is very much worth the try. We are, indeed, "gambling with passions," and in fact rather than just in play. Anything that can provide us with a better sense of the odds we face (which as Damon Runyon once said, are always three-to-two against) is all to the good.

DALE EICKELMAN

As Dale points out, my 1960s writings on Islam—*The Religion of Java, Islam Observed,* and various articles and reviews—were very much of their time and place, not just in terms of history as such, as is inevitable, but in terms of what sort of thing was then being written by "orientalist" scholars. That decade was a rather special time both in the human sciences, especially those like anthropology still concerned with religion, and in the world at large. It was in the full midst of the Cold War, as well as of course, the time of the Vietnam crisis. And it was before the rise—or, at least, before the rise to general view—of what came later to be known as "political" (or "radical," or "fundamentalist" or "extremist") Islam. If there was any reigning view, indeed if there was any general view of Islam at all, in Western minds, it was that it was a relic religion, stiffened, unmodern, and soon to dissolve in the face of some combination of nationalism, secularism, and Marxism. Nationalism, in particular, was, as Nasserism, Baathism, etc., on the march in the Middle East and North Africa, and the role of Islam there was barely on anyone's radar, a few, secluded world-history type scholars like Marshall Hodgson aside. Most students of "the third world" considered it a spent force, a drag on modernity, an "obstacle" to development, to the point that when, a few years further on, this view was finally seen to be (how shall I put it?) inadequate, there was much talk among the same people of "the return of Islam," as though—Indian Partition, The Kuala Lumpur Riots, The Egyptian Brotherhood—it had ever been away.

It was, then, in that general environment, that my earlier work in the field was done. In the Terry Lectures, published as *Islam Observed,* I argued, first, that Islam was indeed alive and well in the two countries I had been studying, Indonesia and Morocco, if only you knew where to look for it in their societies, in their political institutions and among their leading personalities, and if you were willing to turn away from a hypertextualist, Qur'an, Hadith, and Shari'a approach to the matter. Second, by comparing these incomparables, a Southeast Asian, Malayo-Polynesian–based society and a North African Berber one, a number of things would come into view otherwise not so easy to see. In particular, the importance of what I call "scripturalism," and others called "modernism," or "reformism" ("fundamentalism," was not yet, fortunately, the term of art for political Islam) in the nationalist politics of the two countries.

As Dale also notes, time has both reinforced this more dispersive, variegated view of "Islam," and transcended it. We are, right now, in the process of constructing, rather hurriedly as though we had better quickly get on with it after years of neglect, a more contemporary, more realistic, less stereotypical, "postnationalist" view of "Islam." There is, just now, an avalanche of books and articles—by historians, by journalists, by political scientists, by students of contemporary religion, by sociologists and anthropologists, and by various inspired amateurs designed to give us a crash-course in, as the phrase goes, "Understanding Islam." Particularly since 9/11/01 the multiperspective, multidisciplinary approach to Islam one could only hope for and briefly illustrate in the 1960s is dramatically underway, and indeed flying off in all directions, as everyone from Oriana Fallaci to Bay Area Sufis like Stephen Schwartz puts a word in. As for me, used to working along the edges of world history and suddenly engulfed in its center, I am both pleased and nonplussed. Pleased, because what I wanted to have done and could only barely indicate is coming to be done. Nonplussed because what Dale rightly calls my "high risk venture" (he is not correct, however, just for the record, in saying *Islam Observed* was written before I had done fieldwork in Morocco; also, he is wrong about how long one can cling to a glass of Scotch in an airplane—I have tried it) seems even more risky now, as he, Larry Rosen, Bob Hefner, and others take it up, than ever.

ROBERT LEVINE

Robert LeVine is quite right: I will never write a book called *Principia Semiotica,* and am quite astonished to think that someone once imagined I might. The longer I go on, the shorter my books get and the more they decline into essays. But he is right, of course, that something like symbolic action has always been the central subject of my work and that this implied some strong theses in psychology that I was, as is my wont, strongly disinclined to state explicitly. The metaphorics, so to speak, of psychology and psychoanalysis reverberate through my work, not only in the experience-near, experience-distant borrowing from Heinz Kohut, but *The Interpretation of Cultures* was not so named for nothing. It was just that when I began writing the culture-and-personality vocation was so strong and so, as I put it in a recent paper, explanatorily ambitious that I rather shied away. Too much was being said about too many, and it was that—Yurok salmon orality, Russian teeth, swaddling totalitarianism— that rather put me off. Not any antipathy, which as Bob rightly says I never have had, to the subjective and to psychology as such. Now that a properly cultural psychology, grounded in what people actually say and do, rather that in destiny-in-the-nursery (or, later, in programs-in-the-head) abstractions, has been revived by the likes of him, Jerry Bruner, Byron Good and Mary-Jo DelVecchio Good, Rick Shweder, and others, I am, as I think some of my more recent writings testify, more than willing to get back into the effort. And, as he also says, the proper totemic figure for that is Sapir, under the influence of whose writings I began, a half century or so ago now, to think seriously about "symbolic action" and the sort of psychological assumptions it implied.

BYRON GOOD AND MARY-JO DELVECCHIO GOOD

As I mentioned in my comment on Michael Fischer's paper, hanging around long enough to see your successors arrive is much of a mixed blessing. But here, with Byron and Mary-Jo, it is even more shaking. For they have been working—how dare they?—in "my" field site, with "my" people, and "my" culture for the last decade or so. Every field anthropologist, I am sure, wakes up from time to time in a cold sweat fearing that someone has gone back to where he or she worked and found not only that the people had been glad to see the last of him but also that he had made up everything, misquoted everybody, was lied to continuously, and didn't have a clue about what was going on around him. In my case, a supposed American friend, a political scientist, visited Pare, "my" town in east-central Java, for a day about thirty years ago and found that all dozen or so of us who had been there together in the 1950s had been amalgamated in the local Durkheimian memory into a single archetypal figure called "Don," the one proper name (that of the sociologist among us) they could, apparently most easily get their phonemes around. I went back not long after that for a revisit myself and more or less straightened all that out. But my demythologizing efforts were hampered a bit by the fact that one of my oldest friends there and ex-party-chieftain, by then pushing eighty, had just got hold of my book on the history of the place in Indonesian translation, had gone through it and written in the real names of the people, including himself, to whom I had given pseudonyms in an effort to spare them embarrassment, Xeroxed the particular pages involved, and distributed them to the particular people concerned. This provided a re-entry problem (though, as at least at that time and that place "the Javanese were still Javanese," everyone was quite polite about it all) of a peculiar quality. You can't, really can't, go home again.

So far as Byron and Mary-Jo's piece is concerned, they of course have been mainly working in Jogjakarta, where I spent the first eight months of my own expedition in 1952, at a time when it was all oxcarts and bicycles and batiks and hierarchy, and dance classes in the *kraton* (the castle) on Sunday morning. *Pelan-pelan,* "slow, slow" as we used to say; *mboten wonten menapa menapa*—"nothing, absolutely is happening, has happened, or is going to happen." It is very much not like that now of course—it is enormously sprawled out, crowded with honking automobiles, a major university center with students from all over the archipelago. (I have heard people say that half the town's population is now non-Javanese; "nobody stays where they belong anymore.")

So the question, "are the Javanese still Javanese?" is a natural one to raise. In one sense, of course they are; what else could they be? But in another, as Java 1952 and Java 2002 are hardly the same place, uncritically applying conceptions based on experiences trafficking with the first to realities encountered confronting the second is not going to work out very well. So the flow of history presents, in and of itself, a difficult question: What persists? (Because, as the Javanese are still not Americans, Moroccans, or even Bataks, something, and something central surely, does.) And what does not? (Because equally surely, now that "development," massacre, and the state ideologization of culture has intervened, a lot, also central, does not.) After all, as the Goods point out, thirty-five years of Suharto's putting Javanism and Javanist tradition to the most instrumental and oppressive uses, when he finally falls, what do we get in place of him? First, Gus Dur, a Muslim folk figure out of the traditionalist Islamist context of East Javanese madrasah life, and, when he self-destructs, Megawati Sukarnoputri, a Javanese "Ibu" ("mother") whole and entire, complete with grand formality, unnerving patience, and Delphic silences. This is not just the old cliché about change and sameness. It is that this whole question seems to me one of the central perplexities of anthropological accounting: How, through the greatest and most destructive of upheavals, violence, outside intrusion, "modernization"—*dangdut* in a *hijab,* and all that—the core of something, stretched, bent, twisted like a topologist's rubber sheet, perhaps, re-emerges, snaps back, or approximately, into position.

The relation of subjectivity to culture, as the Goods put it, is surely the route to take in attempting to get somewhere with this issue. My own attempt, as limited as it was, to take a phenomenological approach to self and identity questions was, of course, in the first instance stimulated by the Javanese themselves who, at least as I knew them, had a tremendous bent in that direction and could talk about feelings, consciousness, the inner life, and so on (including "psychosomatic" illness) till the water buffaloes came home. "Exploring the new forms of Javanese subjectivity, emerging under ('quite new?' well, anyway 'new') conditions" is clearly the way to go and in doing so the one thing I feel quite sure after all these years is that the Javanese themselves will be superb and willing guides in pursuing such an enterprise. It is hard to get a word out edgewise from the Balinese about what is going on *dalem,* "inside." It is, it still is, hard, so far as I can see, to get the Javanese to stop talking about it.

As for Byron and Mary-Jo's memories of that last year of mine at

Chicago, I can only say I myself had quite forgotten, I suppose repressed, it. Their invocation of how I taught, if "overwhelm with references so they may think you know something" can be called teaching, brought it all back with a rush, and stimulated the same sort of question about my consciousness as needs to be asked about the Javanese. Yes, that person was me. Have I changed? Have I learned anything? Have I unlearned anything?

JEROME BRUNER

As Jerome Bruner notes, he and I go way back, to the caveman times of neo-anti-mentalism, computational determinism, tachistoscopes, and other Harvard horrors. I first encountered him there (but not he, me: I cowered in the back row of a large auditorium, frantically scribbling) in my very first semester in graduate school—that would be 1950—when I audited, because someone said it would be amusing, a course he and the Berkeley experimentalist David Krechevsky, become Krech, gave on perception in which they argued, *mirabile dictu,* that it was *people*—poor kids, rich kids, beggarmen, thieves—who heard and saw, not ears and eyeballs. It was a revelation, as well as one can see clearly now but could already half-sense then, the opening gun in the Cognitive Revolution. The tokening tremors before The Big One. I can still see him in my mind's eye, weaving about the stage like a featherweight boxer, a study in restlessness, energy, rapidity, and thinking, as he came, himself, later to put it, with the jabbing, feinting, cutting left hand.

Since then we have gone our separate ways institutionally, our converging ones intellectually, blaming each other, and Kenneth Burke, for everything that has happened since. "Cultural psychology"/"interpretive anthropology"—bricoleur inventions, each of us annoying our maternal (or are they paternal?) disciplines with each other's arguments. The making of meaning-making. The culturalification of fact, law, and verdict passing. Hermeneutic circles, hermeneutic spirals. Going beyond the information given. It's been a grand ride. Worthy indeed of narration.

NATALIE DAVIS

The interaction between Natalie and myself has been steady and, I think, mutually transforming during the many years we were together in Princeton, she at the university, myself at the Institute. She and I taught a seminar together a couple times that Robert Darnton, another French

historian, and I started sometime in the 1980s on "history and anthropology." In that seminar we confronted the students (juniors and seniors
from various departments—English, International Relations, Art, Economics, History, Anthropology) with paralleled classic texts from both
disciplines: Evans-Prichard and Keith Thomas on witchcraft, Mary Douglas on the Lele and Emmanuel Le Roi Ladurie on the Cathars, Geertz
on Balinese selfhood, Davis on Martin Guerre—to get the students, and
ourselves as well, reflecting on the similarities and differences, both profound, between these two sorts of cousinly minds. I am not sure either
we or the students ever arrived at any very certain position concerning
the matter, because there is no certain position to be reached. But we did
manage to shake up the students as well as ourselves, and a number of
the alumni have gone on to have distinguished interdisciplinary careers,
falling between two, or even three, stools with an aplomb I like to think
owes something to their time with us and our own identity problems.

In her comment, Natalie returns to that old problem: the supposed syn-
chronic, narrow-focus, talking-informants nature of anthropology, and
the (equally supposed) diachronic, wide-lens, dumb-documents nature of
history, and shows again its wild inadequacy in distinguishing the sort of
things she (or Darnton, or Carlo Ginsburg) does from the sort of thing
I (or Douglas, or Ruth Benedict) do. The recurrence in my own work
of temporal images—flowing streams, successive styles, Java or Morocco
then and now—and in her own of configurational ones—patterns of gift-
giving, of being female, of "rough music" for newlyweds in early modern
Europe—pretty well upsets any distinctions based on such matters. Whatever it is that divides history and anthropology, if anything does except
the sheer fact of tradition and university organization, it is not that the one
concerns itself with time and change and the other with form and order.

Prodded then, by Natalie's over-kind comments, to think again about
the differences that connect us, I reflect on the fact that historians, whether
of her sort or Fernand Braudel's Ginsburg's or Lawrence Stone's (another
old Princeton friend of both of us, much missed as both colleague and
foil), write about things that have already reached a certain completion,
things we know the sequel of, how they came out, how they look after they have happened. Anthropologists, whether of my sort or E-P's
or James Fernandez's or Lévi-Strauss's, write about peoples and places
and conditions of things in the midst of happening, whose endings are
as obscured from us as they are from our subjects. For someone such
as myself, concerned with two countries, Morocco and Indonesia, in the
full flow of modern history, this produces a chronic sense of the ground

shifting under your feet: merely in the time to publication your best ideas can be shown to have been quite mistaken, the principles you thought you saw at work been dramatically undercut. Again, this won't really do as a difference marker (there is, after all, Douglas on the ancient Hebrews, Hans Blumenberg on the modern age), but it does at least mark a certain aspect of my own subjectivity in these matters. But all that imagery of flowing rivers and crossing streams, of how it seemed then and how it looks now, comes from a mind haunted by the fact that his subject is changing, and quite rapidly, even as he writes. Historians' books go out of date too, but usually not before they are published. Trying to keep up with world-historical places in an age of world-historical motion gives a certain quality to your prose and a penchant for devices—concentration on a walled town, a prince or a peddler, a market system—that can soften, a bit and incompletely, the anxiety not so much of getting it wrong (that never goes away) but of being seen to have gotten it wrong even as you assert it. Writing history in the midst of history is indeed nervous-making and evasion-producing. But as I say, Natalie would probably counter that things are not all that different in her field.

Also I should perhaps remark on my sense of continuity in my work that she says, surprising me, surprises her. Aside from the fact that we all perhaps look back on our lives in ways that make them look at least minimally directed and should not be taken as authorities on ourselves, part of the problem is that I didn't come to "the study of meaning" after turning away from my initial focus on fact and function. I started out, after my undergraduate work in philosophy and literature, where I was concerned with "the meaning of meaning" and the like on quite supernal levels, went cold-turkey into anthropology and into the field, wrote my licensing volumes, and then took up again, more explicitly (I had never really dropped them, just concealed them in some thick ethnography) the issues about meaning. My career really began in 1946 when I went to college but of course didn't publish anything; which can give the optical illusion of a sea change in the 1970s when the *Interpretation of Cultures* (most of whose articles were written earlier) came out. *Plus ca change, plus c'est le meme auteur.*

AMELIE RORTY

It is appropriate for me to end my so brief, so inadequate, so self-protective series of comments with Amelie's piece, because, in her gadfly, philosophical way, she asks: Ok, Buster—now that you have been duly celebrated, what are you going to do next? As, she would expect, I am inclined to answer: who the hell knows? It's all up for grabs.

But she has, alas, grasped, with uncomfortable exactness, the Yeatsian ("perfection of the life vs. perfection of the work") thematic in my authorial tome, the place where biography, the life I have lived, and representation, the world I have described, meet and clash. Am I, after all, a celebrant of chance or possessed by a rage for order? And, as she suggests, I am both, in unstable, indefensible, and determined imbalance. Everything *is* up for grabs, but we must, somehow, hang on.

To become a bit biographical for a short moment, my actual life, the one that has gone on out there and back then where things happen and happened, has been, in fact, rather a looking for small bits of order to hang onto in the midst of chaos. So it is hardly to wonder that my work looks like a grasping for patterns in a swirl of change: I was preadapted. My parents were divorced when I was three, and I was dispatched (the verb is appropriate) to live alone with an older woman, a nonrelative, amid the sylvan beauties of the northern California countryside (a "nonvillage" of three or four hundred farmers, shopkeepers, and summer visitors) in the plumb depths of the Great Depression. I was well cared for, but that's about it, and I was pretty much left to put my life together (not without real help from schoolteachers responding to a bright kid, and, later on, the U.S. Navy, responding to a callow klutz) by myself. Without going on—I do not much like the "Rosebud" approach to self-understanding—all this predisposed me to becoming, in both life and work, the seeker after a pattern, however fragmentary, amid a swirl of accident, however pervasive, that Amelie rightly sees. It has never occurred to me, not really being a deep thinker, just a nervous one, to try to resolve this "binary." I have just sought to live with it. Pitched early into things, I assumed, and I still assume, that what you are supposed to do is keep going with whatever you can find lying about to keep going with: to get from yesterday to today without foreclosing tomorrow. And it does, that resolute irresolution, indeed show in my work.

I can hardly here really face up to Amelie's challenge to make my conception of the relation between "the dramas of happenstance" and "the plenitude . . . of significant pattern" clear and explicit. I can hardly face up to it at all, save through further fumbling after meaning of the sort I have done in Bali, in Java, in Morocco, in life. Even as such, this sort of seeing openness and order in the same optic has some use, or so I think, as a guide for the perplexed. That philosophical sociologist, David Reisman, once wrote somewhere that the central problem of political life was how to avoid being forced to choose between murder and martyrdom. Good advice in general, and again most especially at the moment, late February 2003, in which I write.

I really don't believe that "everything, but absolutely everything, has a place in a significant order." I just think that some things seem to have some sort of place in a partial sort of order. Bali is not a cockfight writ large, or vice versa. The world is indeed a suq, but the suq is not the world. "Existential anxiety," early encountered, is, for me, apparently here to stay; and, though as Amelie says about Berlin and Taylor, two other passionate evaders, it won't really do, I shall just have to go on, at least so long as chance permits and pattern lasts, "cliffhanging."

Appendixes

APPENDIX 2. ACADEMIC BIOGRAPHY AND WRITINGS OF CLIFFORD GEERTZ

Clifford Geertz
School of Social Science
Institute for Advanced Study
Princeton, New Jersey 08540

Born August 23, 1926, San Francisco, California

FORMAL TRAINING
AB Antioch College, 1950 (Philosophy)
PhD Harvard University, 1956 (Anthropology) Department of Social
  Relations

PROFESSIONAL CAREER
Instructor in Social Relations and Research Associate in the Laboratory
  of Social Relations, Harvard University, 1956–57.
Research Assistant, Center for International Studies, Massachusetts
  Institute of Technology, 1952–56; Research Associate, 1957–58.
Fellow, Center for Advanced Study in the Behavioral Sciences, Stanford,
  California, 1958–59.
Assistant Professor of Anthropology, University of California, Berkeley,
  1958–60.
Assistant Professor of Anthropology, University of Chicago, 1960–61;
  Associate Professor, 1962–64; Professor, 1964–68. Divisional
  Professor in the Social Sciences, 1968–70.
Member of the Committee for the Comparative Study of New Nations,
  University of Chicago, 1962–70; Executive Secretary, 1964–66;
  Chairman, 1968–70.
Senior Research Career Fellow, National Institute of Mental Health,
  1964–70.
Consultant to the Ford Foundation on Social Sciences in Indonesia,
  1971.
Professor of Social Science, Institute for Advanced Study, Princeton,
  New Jersey, 1970–. (Harold F. Linder Professor of Social Science,
  1982–). Professor Emeritus, 2000–.
Visiting Lecturer with Rank of Professor, Department of History,
  Princeton University, 1975–2000.
Eastman Professor, Oxford University, 1978–79.

FIELDWORK

Java, Indonesia, 1952–54; April 1984; March–August 1986;
    November–December 1999.

Bali, Indonesia, 1957–58.

Morocco, June–July 1963; June–December 1964; June 1965–September
    1966; June 1968–April 1969; June–July 1972; June–July 1976;
    November 1985–March 1986.

Java, Bali, Celebes, Sumatra, April–September 1971.

PROFESSIONAL HONORS

A. Honorary Degrees

Honorary Doctor of Laws, Harvard University, 1974.

Honorary Doctor of Humane Letters, Northern Michigan University,
    1975.

Honorary Doctor of Humane Letters, University of Chicago, 1979.

Honorary Doctor of Humane Letters, Bates College, 1980.

Honorary Doctor of Humane Letters, Knox College (Illinois), 1982.

Honorary Doctor of Humane Letters, Brandeis University, 1984.

Honorary Doctor of Humane Letters, Swarthmore College, 1984.

Honorary Doctor of Humane Letters, New School for Social Research,
    1987.

Honorary Doctor of Social Science, Yale University, 1987.

Honorary Doctor of Letters, Williams College, 1991.

Honorary Doctor of Humane Letters, Princeton University, 1995.

Honorary Doctor of Letters, University of Cambridge, 1997.

Honorary Doctor of Letters, Georgetown University, 1998.

Honorary Doctor of Letters, Antioch College, 1999.

Honorary Doctor of Laws, Colby College, 2003.

B. Scholarly Awards

Social Science Prize (Talcott Parsons Prize), American Academy of Arts
    and Sciences, 1974.

Sorokin Prize, American Sociological Association, 1974.

Distinguished Lecturer, American Anthropological Association, 1983.

Huxley Memorial Lecturer and Medallist, Royal Anthropological
    Institute, 1983.

Distinguished Scholar Award, Association for Asian Studies, 1987.

National Book Critics Circle Prize in Criticism, 1988.

Horace Mann Distinguished Alumnus Award, Antioch College, 1992.

Fukuoka Asian Cultural Prize (Academic, International), 1992.

Bintang Jasa Utama (Medal), Republic of Indonesia, 2002.

C. *Scholarly Memberships*

Fellow, American Academy of Arts and Sciences, 1966–.
Fellow, Council on Foreign Relations, 1970–.
Fellow, American Philosophical Society, 1972–.
Fellow, The National Academy of Sciences, 1973–.
Fellow, American Association for the Advancement of Science, 1980–.
Corresponding Fellow, The British Academy, 1991–.
Honorary Fellow, The Royal Anthropological Institute of Great Britain and Ireland, 1995–.

D. *Lectureships*

Terry Lecturer, Yale University, 1967.
Harry F. Camp Memorial Lecturer, Stanford University, 1972.
John Dewey Lecturer, Antioch College, 1973.
Lionel Trilling Lecturer, Columbia University, 1977.
Storrs Lecturer, Yale Law School, 1981.
Bicentennial Lecturer, American Academy of Arts and Sciences, 1981.
Harry F. Camp Memorial Lecturer, Stanford University, 1983.
Obert C. Tanner Lecturer, University of Michigan, 1985.
Lindesmith Lecturer, Carleton College, 1990.
Hitchcock Lecturer, University of California, 1990.
Harvard-Jerusalem Lecturer, 1990.
Hardy Lecturer, Hartwick College, 1992.
Fukuoka Five-Year Anniversary Lecturer, Tokyo and Fukuoka, 1995.
Lecturer in Modern Philosophy, Institut für die Wissenschaften vom Menschen, Vienna, 1995.
William James Lecturer, Harvard Divinity School, 1998.
Wells Lecturer, University of Indiana, 1998.
Charles Homer Haskins Lecturer, American Council of Learned Societies, 1999.
Master's Seminar, University of Konstanz, 2000.
Sabbagh Lecturer, University of Arizona, 2001.
Sidney A. Mintz Lecturer, Johns Hopkins University, 2003.
Sir James Frazer Lecturer, University of Cambridge, 2004.

E. *Other*

Council of Scholars, Library of Congress, 1982–93.
Fellow, Intellectual Interchange Program, Japan Society, 1984.
Visiting Fellow, Humanities Research Centre, Australian National University, 1987.
Rector's Visitor, Wissenschaftskolleg zu Berlin, Germany, 1993.
Visiting Professor, European University Institute, Florence, Italy, 1994.

Visiting Scholar, EHESS, Paris, 1994.

Visiting Scholar, Getty Research Institute for the History of Art and the Humanities, 1998.

BIBLIOGRAPHY

For a complete bibliography together with translations and reprints, see I. Mörth and G. Fröhlich, HyperGeertz World Catalogue, online at http://www.iwp.uni-linz.ac.at/lxe/sektktf/gg/HyperGeertz.html.

BOOKS

The Religion of Java. Glencoe, IL: Free Press, 1960.

(Editor). *Old Societies and New States.* New York: Free Press, 1963.

Agricultural Involution, the Processes of Ecological Change in Indonesia. Berkeley: University of California Press, 1963.

Peddlers and Princes. Chicago: University of Chicago Press, 1963.

The Social History of an Indonesian Town. Cambridge: MIT Press, 1965.

Person, Time, and Conduct in Bali: An Essay in Cultural Analysis. Yale Southeast Asia Program Cultural Report Series, no. 14, 1966.

Islam Observed: Religious Development in Morocco and Indonesia. New Haven: Yale University Press, 1968.

The Interpretation of Cultures: Selected Essays. New York: Basic Books, 1973, 2000.

(Editor). *Myth, Symbol and Culture.* New York: Norton, 1974.

(with Hildred Geertz). *Kinship in Bali.* Chicago: University of Chicago Press, 1975.

(with Hildred Geertz and Lawrence Rosen). *Meaning and Order in Moroccan Society.* New York: Cambridge University Press, 1979.

Negara: The Theatre State in Nineteenth Century Bali. Princeton: Princeton University Press, 1980.

Local Knowledge: Further Essays in Interpretive Anthropology. New York: Basic Books, 1983, 2000.

Bali, interprétation d'une culture. Paris: Editions Gallimard, 1983.

Works and Lives: The Anthropologist as Author. Stanford: Stanford University Press, 1988.

After the Fact: Two Countries, Four Decades, One Anthropologist. Cambridge: Harvard University Press, 1995.

Welt in Stücken: Kultur und Politik am Ende des 20. Jahrhunderts: Passagen Verlag, 1996.

Available Light: Anthropological Reflections on Philosophical Topics.
  Princeton: Princeton University Press, 2000.
The Politics of Culture, Asian Identities in a Splintered World
  (Japanese). Tokyo: Misuzu Shobo, 2002.

ARTICLES

1956
"Religious Belief and Economic Behavior in a Central Javanese Town:
  Some Preliminary Considerations." *Economic Development and
  Cultural Change,* 2: 134–58.
"Capital-Intensive Agriculture in Peasant Society: A Case Study." *Social
  Research,* Winter: 433–49.

1957
"Ritual and Social Change: A Javanese Example." *American
  Anthropologist,* 59: 32–54.

1958
"Ethos, World View, and the Analysis of Sacred Symbols." *Antioch
  Review,* Winter: 421–37.

1959
"The Javanese Village." In G. W. Skinner, ed., *Local Ethnic and
  National Loyalties in Village Indonesia: A Symposium.* New Haven:
  Yale University Southeast Asia Program Cultural Report Series,
  34–41.
"Form and Variation in Balinese Village Structure." *American
  Anthropologist,* 61: 991–1012.

1960
"The Javanese Kijaji: The Changing Role of a Cultural Broker."
  Comparative Studies in Society and History, 2: 228–49.

1962
"Studies in Peasant Life: Community and Society." In B. J. Siegel, ed.,
  Biennial Review of Anthropology 1961. Stanford: Stanford
  University Press, 1–41.
"Social Change and Economic Modernization in Two Indonesian
  Towns: A Case in Point." In E. Hagen, *On the Theory of Social
  Change.* Homewood, IL: Dorsey, 385–410.
"The Rotating Credit Association: A 'Middle Rung' in Development."
  Economic Development and Cultural Change, 10(3): 241–63.

"The Growth of Culture and the Evolution of Mind." In J. Sher, ed., *Theories of the Mind*. New York: Free Press, 713–40.

1963

"The Integrative Revolution: Primordial Sentiments and Civil Politics in the New States." In C. Geertz, ed., *Old Societies and New States*. New York: Free Press, 105–57.

"The Socio-Cultural Context of Policy in Southeast Asia." In W. Henderson, ed., *Southeast Asia: Problems of Policy*. Cambridge: MIT Press, 54–70.

1964

"Ideology as a Cultural System." In D. Apter, ed., *Ideology and Discontent*. New York: Free Press, 47–76.

(with Hildred Geertz). "Teknonymy in Bali: Parenthood, Age-Grading, and Genealogical Amnesia." *Journal of the Royal Anthropological Institute*, 94(part 2): 94–108.

"Tihingan: A Balinese Village," *Bijdragen tot de taal-, land-, en Volkenkunde*, 120: 1–33; and Koentjaraningrat, ed., *Village Communities in Indonesia*, Ithaca and Djakarta: Cornell University Press and University of Indonesia Press, 1966.

"The Transition to Humanity." In S. Tax, ed., *Horizons of Anthropology*. Chicago: Aldine, 37–48.

" 'Internal Conversion' in Contemporary Bali." In J. Bastin and R. Roolvink, eds., *Malay and Indonesian Studies*. Oxford: Oxford University Press, 282–302.

1966

"Modernization in a Muslim Society: The Indonesian Case." In R. N. Bellah, ed., *Religion and Progress in Modern Asia*. New York: Free Press, 93–108.

"Religion as a Cultural System." In M. Banton, ed., *Anthropological Approaches to the Study of Religion*. London: Tavistock, 1–46.

"Are the Javanese Mad?" *Encounter*, August: 86–88.

"The Impact of the Concept of Culture on the Concept of Man." In J. Platt, ed., *New Views of the Nature of Man*. Chicago: University of Chicago Press, 93–118.

1967

"Politics Past, Politics Present: Some Notes on the Contribution of Anthropology to the Study of the New States." *Archives européenes de sociologie*, 8: 1–14.

"The Cerebral Savage: The Structural Anthropology of Claude
Lévi-Strauss." *Encounter,* April.

1968
"Religion, Anthropological Aspects." *International Encyclopedia of the
Social Sciences.* New York: Macmillan.
"Village." *International Encyclopedia of the Social Sciences.* New York:
Macmillan.
"Thinking as a Moral Act: Ethical Dimensions of Anthropological Field
Work in the New States." *Antioch Review,* 27: 134–59.

1969
"Myrdal's Mythology." *Encounter,* July: 26–34.

1971
"After the Revolution: The Fate of Nationalism in the New States." In
A. Inkeles and B. Barber, eds., *Stability and Social Change.*
Cambridge: Harvard University Press, 357–76.
"Afterword: The Politics of Meaning." In C. Holt, ed., *Culture and
Politics in Indonesia.* Ithaca: Cornell University Press, 319–36.
"Deep Play: Notes on the Balinese Cockfight." *Daedalus,* Winter: 1–38.
"Comment." In R. Antoun and I. Harik, eds., *Rural Politics and Social
Change in the Middle East.* Bloomington: Indiana University Press,
460–66.
"The Wet and the Dry: Traditional Irrigation in Bali and Morocco."
Human Ecology, 1: 34–39.
"Introduction." In J. Harrison, ed., *South and Southeast Asia.* Tucson:
University of Arizona Press, v–viii.
"Religious Change and Social Order in Suharto's Indonesia." *Asia,* 27:
62–84.

1973
"Comments on Benjamin White's 'Demand for Labor and Population
Growth in Colonial Java.'" *Human Ecology,* 1: 237.

1974
"Social Science Policy in a New State: A Programme for the Stimulation
of the Social Sciences in Indonesia." *Minerva,* 12: 365–81.

1975
"Common Sense as a Cultural System." *Antioch Review,* 33: 47–53.
"On the Nature of Anthropological Understanding." *American
Scientist,* 63: 47–53. Also in K. Basso and H. Selby, eds., *Approaches*

to Symbolic Anthropology. Albuquerque: University of New Mexico Press, 1976, 221–37.

1976
"Art as a Cultural System." *MLN,* 91: 1473–99.

1977
"Centers, Kings, and Charisma: Reflections on the Symbolics of Power." In J. Ben-David and T. N. Clark, eds., *Culture and Its Creators.* Chicago: University of Chicago Press, 150–71.
"Foreword." In G. Witherspoon, *Language and Art in the Navajo Universe.* Ann Arbor: University of Michigan Press, vii–x.
"Found in Translation: On the Social History of the Moral Imagination." *Georgia Review,* 31: 787–810.
"The Judging of Nations: Some Comments on the Assessment of Regimes in the New States." *Archives européennes de sociologie,* 18: 245–61.

1978
"The Bazaar Economy: Information and Search in Peasant Marketing." *American Economic Review,* 68(2): 28–32.

1979
"Suq: The Bazaar Economy in Sefrou." In C. Geertz, H. Geertz, and L. Rosen, *Meaning and Order in Moroccan Society.* New York: Cambridge University Press.

1980
"Blurred Genres: The Refiguration of Social Thought." *American Scholar,* 49(2): 165–79.
"Ports of Trade in Nineteenth Century Bali." In G. Dalton, ed., *Research in Economic Anthropology,* vol. 3. Greenwich, CT: JAI Press, 109–22.

1982
"The Way We Think Now: Toward an Ethnography of Modern Thought." *Bulletin, The American Academy of Arts and Sciences,* 35(5): 14–34.
"Foreword." In K. Pelzer, *Planters against Peasants.* Leiden: KITLV, vii–xi.

1983
"Slide Show: Evans-Pritchard's African Transparencies." *Raritan,* Fall: 62–80.

"Foreword." In J. Stephen Lansing, *The Three Worlds of Bali.* New York: Praeger, vii–x.

"Foreword." In L. Gesick, ed., *Centers, Symbols, and Hierarchies: Essays on the Classical States of Southeast Asia.* New Haven: Yale University Southeast Asia Studies, Monograph Series, no. 26, viii–x.

1984

"Anti Anti-Relativism." *American Anthropologist,* 86(2): 263–78.

"Culture and Social Change: The Indonesian Case." *Man,* 19: 511–32.

"Introduction." In D. F. Eickelman, *Knowledge and Power: Religious Intellectuals in Rural Morocco.* Princeton: Princeton University Press, xi–xiv.

1985

"Waddling In." *Times Literary Supplement,* June 7, 1985, 623–24.

1986

"Epilogue: Making Experiences, Authoring Selves." In V. W. Turner and E. Bruner, eds., *The Anthropology of Experience.* Urbana: University of Illinois Press, 373–80.

"The Uses of Diversity." *Michigan Quarterly Review,* 25(1): 105–23. Also in *Tanner Lectures on Human Values,* vol. 7. Salt Lake City: University of Utah Press, 253–75.

1988

"Recollections of an Itinerant Career." (Jamie Mackie, interviewer). *Bulletin of Indonesian Economic Studies,* 24: 1–18.

1989

"Margaret Mead." In *Biographical Memoirs,* vol. 58. Washington, DC: National Academy Press, 328–54.

"Toutes Directions: Reading the Signs in an Urban Sprawl." *International Journal of Middle Eastern Studies,* 21: 291–306.

1990

"History and Anthropology." *New Literary History,* 21: 321–35.

" 'Popular Art' and the Javanese Tradition." *Indonesia,* October. Also in A. Gerstle and A. Milner, eds., *Recovering the Orient: Artists, Scholars, Appropriations.* London: Harwood Academic Publishers, 1994, 245–67.

1991

"The Social Scientist as Author: Clifford Geertz on Ethnography and

Social Construction." (Gary Olson, interviewer). *Journal of Advanced Composition,* 11: 245–68.

"An Interview with Clifford Geertz." (Richard Handler, interviewer). *Current Anthropology,* 32: 603–13.

"Lévi-Strauss Self-Inscribed." *Common Knowledge,* 1: 129–34.

1992

"Achter de Feiten: Twee Landen, Vier Decennia, Één Antropoloog." In C. Bouw and B. Kruithof, eds., *De Kern van het Verschil: Culturen en Identiteiten.* Amsterdam: Amsterdam University Press, 41–58.

"Introduction" to "Symposium: Exit from the Balkans—the Commensuration of Alien Languages," 10–12, and " 'Ethnic Conflict': Three Alternative Terms." *Common Knowledge,* 2(3): 54–65.

1993

"Préface." In H. Elboudrari, ed., *Modes de transmission de la culture religieuse en Islam.* Cairo: Institut français d'archéologie orientale.

" 'Local Knowledge' and Its Limits: Some Obiter Dicta." *Yale Journal of Criticism,* 5: 129–35.

1994

"Preface." In K. Newland and K. Soedjatmoko, *Transforming Humanity: The Visionary Writings of Soedjatmoko.* West Hartford, CT: Kumarian Press, vii–x.

"Foreword." In Gary A. Olson, ed., *Philosophy, Rhetoric, Literary Criticism: (Inter)views.* Carbondale: Southern Illinois University Press, xi–xii.

1995

"The Strange Estrangement: Taylor and the Natural Sciences." In James Tully, ed., *Philosophy in an Age of Pluralism.* Cambridge: Cambridge University Press, 83–95.

"Disciplines." *Raritan,* Winter: 65–102.

"Reason, Religion, and Professor Gellner." In H. R. Hoetink, ed., *The Limits of Pluralism: Neo-Absolutism and Relativism.* Amsterdam: Praemium Erasmanium Foundation, 167–72.

1996

"Off Echoes: Some Comments on Anthropology and Law." *PoLAR,* 19(2): 33–37.

"Afterword." In K. Basso and S. Feld, eds., *Senses of Place.* Santa Fe: SAR Press.

1997

"The Legacy of Thomas Kuhn: The Right Text at the Right Time."
Common Knowledge, 6(1): 1–5.

"What Is a Country If It Is Not a Nation?" *Brown Journal of World
Affairs,* 4(2): 235–247.

"Cultural Tourism: Tradition, Identity, and Heritage Construction." In
Wiendu Nuryanti, ed., *Tourism and Heritage Management.*
Jogjakarta: Gadjah Mada University Press, 14–24.

1998

"The World in Pieces." *FOCAAL,* 32: 91–117.

1999

" 'The Pinch of Destiny:' Religion as Experience, Meaning, Identity,
Power." *Raritan,* Winter: 1–19.

"When the Poet Speaks Arabic." *To Be:2B,* 14: 106–7.

"Awas Buaya." In F. X. Baskara J. Wardaya, ed., *Mencari Demokrasi.*
Jakarta: Institut Studi Arus Informasi, 51–94.

"A Life of Learning." ACLS Publications.

"The Introduction into Anthropology of a Genuinely Historical Eye."
Roundtable on George Stocking. *Journal of Victorian Culture,*
305–10.

"Afterword." In R. Demallie, ed., *Interpreting Cultures.* Bloomington:
Indiana University Press.

2000

"Geiger at Antioch." *Antioch Review,* Winter.

"Bruner's Imbalancing Act." In D. Bakhurst and S. Shanker, eds.,
Jerome Bruner: Language, Culture, Self. Thousand Oaks, CA: Sage
Publications.

2001

"School Building: A Retrospective Preface." In J. Scott and D. Keates,
eds., *Schools of Thought: Twenty-Five Years of Interpretive Social
Science.* Princeton: Princeton University Press, 1–11.

2002

"The Near East in the Far East." In F. Pouillon, *Essays for Lucette
Valensi.* Princeton: Institute for Advanced Study, School of Social
Science, Occasional Papers, no. 12, 2001.

"An Inconstant Profession, The Anthropological Life in Interesting
Times." *Annual Review of Anthropology,* 31: 1–19.

"Interview with Clifford Geertz" (N. Panourgia). *Anthropological Theory*, 2(4): 421–31.

"I Don't Do Systems. An Interview with Clifford Geertz" (A. Michaelsen). *Journal of the North American Association for the Study of Religion*, 2–20.

Forthcoming

"Commentary." In R. Shweder and B. Good, eds., *Clifford Geertz by His Colleagues*. Chicago: University of Chicago Press.

"Ritual as a Model System." *Il Perugino*.

"A Fine Romance: Anthropology and Literature." *Current Anthropology*.

"What Is a State If It Is Not a Sovereign: Reflections on Politics in Complicated Places." *Current Anthropology*.

"Shifting Aims, Moving Targets: On the Anthropology of Religion." *Journal of the Royal Anthropological Institute*.

Essay Reviews: *New York Review of Books*

"Under the Mosquito Net," September 14, 1967.

"Gandhi: Non-Violence as Therapy," 1969.

"In Search of North Africa," April 22, 1971.

"Mysteries of Islam," December 11, 1975.

"Stir Crazy," January 26, 1978.

"Sociosexology," January 24, 1980.

"Conjuring with Islam," May 27, 1982.

"The Ultimate Ghetto," February 28, 1985.

"A South Sea Renaissance," February 16, 1989.

"A Lab of One's Own," November 8, 1990.

"Genet's Last Stand," November 19, 1992.

"Life on the Edge," April 7, 1994.

"Culture War," November 30, 1995.

"The New Psychology," April 10, 1997.

"Deep Hanging Out," October 22, 1998.

"Indonesia: Starting Over," May 11, 2000.

"Life among the Anthros," February 8, 2001.

"The Visit," October 18, 2001.

"Gombrich and Primitivism," September 26, 2002.

"Which Way to Mecca?" June 12, July 3, 2003.

ESSAY REVIEWS: *THE NEW REPUBLIC*

"The Forbidden Experiment: The Story of the Wild Boy of Aveyron by Roger Shattuck," April 12, 1980.

"Socialism in Siberia," August 6, 1984.

"The Anthropologist at Large," May 25, 1987.

"The Year of Living Culturally," October 21, 1991.

"Footsteps and House of Glass by Pramoedya Ananta Toer," April 22, 1996.

"Off the Menu," February 17, 2003.

Index

Adorno, Theodor, 81
Alinsky, Saul, 81
Allport, Gordon, 21
American Anthropological Association
    (AAA), vii, ix, 8, 18n23, 36, 53
Anderson, Benedict, 59
anthropology: and astonishment, 91–92;
    cosmopolitanism of, 93, 94–95;
    happenstance and pattern and, 49–51;
    history and, 39, 47, 64, 68, 121–22;
    and interpretation, 11–14, 45; and
    judgment, 7–8, 10, 13–14, 108–9;
    and large issues, 89–95, 112–14; and
    pluralism, 2, 7, 8; social, 57; study
    of religion, 66–68; symbolic, 57–58,
    86–87; "the third stream" of, 60n2; use
    of comparison, 93–94
Antioch College, 49
Appiah, Kwame Anthony, 94
Arendt, Hannah, 86
Aristotle, 13
Arnold, Matthew, 64

Balinese cockfight, 22, 38, 39, 47–48, 54
Balinese ideology of reform (*reformasi*),
    105–6
Bateson, Gregory, 77
Beck, Ulrich, 85–86
Beidelman, T. O., 57
Bellah, Robert, 58, 67
Benedict, Ruth, 13, 41, 53, 95, 121
Benjamin, Walter, 81
Bentham, Jeremy, 31, 81, 114
Berlin, Isaiah, 7–8, 12, 17n10, 50, 51, 110,
    124
Berry, Thomas, 56

Blumenberg, Hans, 122
blurred genres, 76, 79, 82
Boas, Franz, 36n1, 52, 57, 60n2
Boon, James A., 58, 109, 112
Borges, Jorge Luis, 67
Bourdieu, Pierre, 64
Bowen, John, 71, 72
Braudel, Fernand, 121
Brenner, Susanne, 103
Brown, Peter, 72
Bruner, Jerome, 95, 98, 117, 120
Burke, Kenneth, 22, 29, 81, 95, 120
buzkashi, 82–83, 115

Cai, Hua, 12, 16n9
Cassirer, Ernst, 100
Cavafy, C. P., 111
chance. *See* happenstance
Clemens, Samuel. *See* Twain, Mark
coded communication, 25–26
Cohn, Bernard, 63–64, 66
componential analysis, 53, 111
Cornell, Vincent, 72
cosmopolitanism, 93, 94–95
Crabb, David, 58
Crapanzano, Vincent, 17n18
cultural critique, 3–4, 13. *See also* judgment
cultural psychology, viii, 20, 88n1, 98;
    endorsed by Geertz, 117; of Javanese,
    101, 102–4
culture: causal-functional vs. logico-
    meaningful integration, 52, 65, 79,
    111; as coded communication, 25–26;
    concept of, 2, 25–27, 52, 54–60, 68–70,
    72, 92; as symbolic action, 25–26